WHOLE & HOLY
SEXUALITY

*How to Find Human and Spiritual Integrity
as a Sexual Person*

WHOLE & HOLY
SEXUALITY

*How to Find Human and Spiritual Integrity
as a Sexual Person*

William F. Kraft, Ph.D.

No portion of this book may be reproduced in any form without expressed permission of the author and/or publisher.

Cover Design:
Scott Wannemuehler

Library of Congress Catalog Number
88-83364

ISBN 0-87029-222-6

Published by Abbey Press
St. Meinrad Archabbey
St. Meinrad, Indiana 47577

To My Other Half,
Pat

Gratitude

This book could not have been written without the help of clients, students, teachers, colleagues, friends, and family. Specifically, I thank Mom and Dad who gave life to me and formed me, my kids who continually challenge me, my friends who understand and humor me, and my wife who confronts, comforts, tickles, and loves me. I also thank Pat Frauenholz and Toni Aliberti for their tireless typing. In short, I thank you whom I have come to know: women, men, and God.

Table of Contents

Preface

Professionally and personally, I frequently listen to men and women discontented with contemporary models of sexuality. Their frustration is usually directed toward approaches that are either exclusively biological and technological or too philosophical and theological. Emphasizing physical and technical information, the first approach is practical, easily learned, and popular, but it lacks personal depth and a value system that can be used to judge and promote healthy and/or holy sexuality. The second approach, focusing on ethical and moral concerns, offers a vision for living a good and holy life; however, many experience it as too abstract, difficult to follow, and lacking cultural support.

The goal of this book is to integrate these two approaches, the so-called secular and sacred perspectives, and to formulate a model that takes account of the relevant scientific, empirical, and clinical data, as well as the philosophical, spiritual, and pastoral data of human sexuality. It offers an alternative to conventional models of sexuality. Too many of us—adults, adolescents, and children—are formed according to a fragmented rather than a wholistic model of sexuality. For instance, an ethic that models and reinforces sexual license and sexism and presents biological and/or psychosocial aspects of sexuality while minimizing or excluding the spiritual dimension needs to be questioned. And, a model that gives standards for sexual behavior without sufficient empirical or experiential support, or ways to implement these standards, can surely be improved.

Many people today are dissatisfied with the "value-less" and "spirit-less" approach to sexuality that pervades our educational system, mass media, and culture. They want to be true to their values and religious heritage, but lack the educational, clinical, and pastoral help to do so. The question of how to be a good and holy sexual person is not adequately addressed.

Instead of following the customary biological and psychosocial approaches to sexuality, I have chosen a phenomenological approach which integrates the relevant data from experience as well as from biology, psychology, sociology, philosophy, and spirituality. Note that although the spirituality of sexuality is a primary theme, the truths of theology, Scripture, and revelation are not explicitly included—I am a psychologist, not a theologian. Nevertheless, theologians and religious leaders across the theological spectrum have assured me that my vision is not incongruent with theirs and that it can serve as the infrastructure for their own approach.

In short, this book presents a wholistic vision of personhood as the framework for formulating a wholistic theory of sexuality. The structures and dynamics of three basic modes of sexuality— primary, affective, and genital—are presented, as well as their problems and possibilities for healthy and holy growth. Specifically, the sense and nonsense of various experiences of sexuality are analyzed: male-female similarities and differences, heterosexual and homosocial relationships, marital and nonmarital sexual feelings and behaviors, masturbation, pornography, homosexuality, and pedophilia.

I have found that clients, teachers-students, parents-children, and celibate and non-celibate persons desire and respond to an integrative sexuality—one that incorporates their physical, psychosocial, and spiritual dimensions and that offers concrete ways to achieve a healthy and holy sexuality. I hope what follows will help married, single, and vowed celibate people to cope with, grow from, and enjoy sexuality.

CHAPTER 1

Sexual Persons

Consider the reflections of this thirty-five year old woman: "My divorce was the most difficult thing I've ever experienced. The pain for me and my kids, and I think for my husband too, was excruciating. Although I never believed in divorce, I felt that a marriage where people were killing each other was worse than any divorce. Sure, it's easy to say now that I got married when I was too young, nineteen. But we did it—and we had three children.

"It's been three years since my divorce, and things are settling down a bit. I've somehow learned to get by with much less than I previously had, and I'm a little more fortunate than many women because I have a decent job. Still, I might add, I'm not paid nearly the same as a man doing a comparable job. I resent that, but I've learned that pent-up anger does a lot of harm to everyone, especially me. Nevertheless, we are managing, and I feel we are better off.

"Yes, it's difficult, especially when I get lonely. Sometimes I crave to be intimate. Sometimes my desires seem purely physical—almost anybody will do. Usually, I want to be close, to touch, to be with someone who loves me. I've had two relationships in the past two years. No, I don't go down to a bar to be picked up, though I can appreciate women who do this. I met a couple of nice guys who honestly proposed—and I agreed—that we would have a short-term relationship while we enjoyed and appreciated each other. We had fun; it really was good to be touched and to touch. The relationship was not all sexual, but sex was part of it.

"When we separated I felt disappointment and pain, but this was our agreement, so it eased the pain. But am I destined to go through life having periodic . . . affairs? I hate to call them that;

it sounds cheap. They're more than that. But when the relationship is over, I have to admit that I feel empty and depressed. It seems that nothing lasts. Must I be condemned to being lonely and alone?

"I have few qualms about getting married again. But this time I'm going to be sure; I'll try to know what I'm getting into. Still, I'm thirty-five; I'm not old, but I'm not young either. Try to get married when you have three kids and you're over thirty. Sure, I suppose you can get married if you're willing to get married to almost anyone, but I don't want to travel that road again.

"I really don't know what's going to happen; it scares me. I want to get married, but I want to have a good and happy marriage. I feel the odds are against this. So what do I do? Do I try to raise my kids and periodically have some sort of relationship? Do I try to be a single mother? Do I masturbate when my needs become intense? Believe me, masturbation is a poor substitute for another person. Can you tell me where I can find an available mature man? Can you tell me what I should do with my yearnings for intimacy? One is a lonely number. Should I just accept my lot and live through it? Life is too short for that. What should I do? Can you tell me?"

This woman does not want to be single; she finds herself in a quandary. Although her relationships give short-term meaning and satisfaction, they fail to promote sustained serenity and growth. Although she desires and enjoys sex, she wants steadfast love even more. She also knows she is growing older, and pressures, often sexist, are against her. She chooses to be divorced in lieu of a marital charade, yet she does not want to be single. What chance does she really have? If she remains single, what can she do with her longing for intimacy?

"My parents were not exactly thrilled when I told them I planned to become a nun. They knew I was thinking about entering religious life, but they never thought I would go through with it. Of course, they said they wanted what was best for me, but my plans seemed to disappoint them.

"They asked if I really knew what I was doing. Was I willing to give up married life, a husband, and children? My father bluntly asked me if I could be happy and celibate. My first impulse was to confront them with the realities of married life. I wanted to ask them how many married people are really happy and fulfilled. I wanted to say that married life is often no big deal. But I didn't verbalize these questions. I was convinced that religious life was the best way for me to live and to love.

"My older brother shook his head in apparent disgust; my younger sister thought I was stupid. Some relatives gave me lukewarm approval, but others just seemed indifferent. My friends pointed out the fun and opportunities I would be missing. The guy I was dating was really shocked at first. Although he knew it was coming, he was hurt. And my decision hurt me, too; I still hurt when I think about us. But if I didn't at least give the religious life a try, I felt I'd be doing myself and him an injustice. I didn't say much, only that I loved him but couldn't marry him.

"All that seems like a thousand years ago now; it was twenty-five years ago. A silver jubilee evokes such memories. Religious life has been good to me; I hope I have been good to it. I have precious friends. I think I've given good service. More importantly, I feel I've grown closer to God and to people. But my father's haunting question comes back to me: can I really live a celibate life? The experts say I'm at the peak of my sexual life, and I believe them. I'm at a loss about what to do with my sexual feelings. Sometimes when I'm lonely, I yearn to hold a man and be held by him. I admit that I wonder what it would be like to make love with a man. Although I know this is contrary to my commitment, I still have my yearnings to be intimate, my desires to give and to be given to.

"Yes, I know the latest theories encourage integrating sexuality. But they don't say how. Integration is a nice word; how in God's name do you do it? I tried masturbation, but that really didn't do any good. It relieved some tension, but it seemed to make things worse. Besides, I feel uncomfortable with masturbation. I don't have the guilt feelings I had when I was an adolescent, but I sense masturbation is not the best way to cope with my sexuality. After masturbating, I feel more lonely.

"I am trying to lead a good religious life, and many people say that I do. I am a celibate for the kingdom of God, but I am also sexual—very much so. Sometimes I feel I am the only one like me, but I know most sisters have the same feelings as I do to a greater or lesser degree. Still, we seldom if ever talk about it.

Sure, we hear lectures and sometimes a few friends will talk
about it a bit, but seldom are the cards put on the table and something concrete done about it. I feel so alone with my sexuality."

Unlike the single parent, this religious sister vowed celibacy.
She believes that a vowed and celibate life in a religious community is the best way she can live. She is a vibrant woman who
loves and serves God and people, but her sexuality is frustrating.
She often finds herself in situations of collusion where everybody pretends to themselves and to others that sexual issues are
unimportant or resolved. Although this sister is given ongoing
spiritual and psychological formation, she feels that the sexual
(incarnational) aspect of her life is given little practical recognition.

"Celibacy—why in the world would somebody choose that?
What do people like nuns, brothers, and priests do with their sexuality? My guess is that some masturbate or mess around; others
repress it and become irritable and frustrated. Really, I don't
know what they do. I don't know how they can be happy or
healthy without sex. Isn't celibacy abnormal? You could call me
a celibate in the sense that I'm not married. But I have an active
sex life; sex is not that difficult to find. There are a lot of lovely
women and there are a lot of places where they are just waiting
to be shown a good time. Besides, increasingly more women are
taking the initiative to have sex and settle for short-term relationships, no strings attached.

"I've been married twice. No more of that for me. Too much
hassle—and for what? If I didn't have these damn payments, I'd
be on easy street. I have my own place, sports car, and I go wher-
ever and whenever I want. What's better than having what you
want?

"Yet, I have to admit that AIDS has changed the ball game,
not only for me but also for others. Everyone is becoming a lot
more careful. Some women bluntly ask if you are a carrier; some
even ask if you have proof to verify your health. Just recently, a
girl refused to have sex with me unless I used a condom, and
even then she made me withdraw before ejaculating. However, I
can see her viewpoint. Times are changin'!

"Okay, I know I'm getting older—I'm fifty-two. I guess I
have to admit I'm not what I used to be. But if you have money

and make the effort, you can get most of what you want. Me lonely? I guess I am sometimes, but who isn't? And of course there's always masturbation. Sure, it's not as good as a woman, but it helps and it's safe. What do I do with my sexuality? What else?—I satisfy it."

This man's life and approach to sex differ radically from the sister and the divorced woman. When he desires sex, he simply finds a woman or he masturbates. With the exception of his concern about AIDS, he claims to have no problems with sex. Although he does not speak of love, he admits to loneliness—the presence of a beloved in absence. We will see that this individual and others like him need and even desire the spiritual, that recreational sex is actually an unconscious but aborted attempt to experience transcendence: healthy union with another.

Consider the thoughts of a sixty-year-old man: "When my wife died, I almost died. It's good to say that we were happy with each other. I am grateful, but I still feel lost and lonely. I am fortunate to have lived with and to have loved such a wonderful woman for thirty-five years, and to have three fine children. Although I know my wife is still with me, I can't really touch and feel, laugh and play with, talk and listen to her. This hurts and hurts and hurts. I feel cheated and get angry when I see people much older than she was. We planned so much and looked forward to enjoying time together in our later years. Why did she die?

"I don't really want to get married again, but I find myself reaching out for someone. I think my wife would understand this. I know I can enter a relationship, short- or long-term. In some ways this would ease my pain. And yet I feel my pain would return more than ever. Sometimes I feel that making love to a woman, almost any woman, would make things better. Sometimes the yearning is intense and I don't know what to do. Alcohol helps, but it only numbs the pain for awhile and solves nothing. When I take stock of myself, I wonder if I am strong enough to be celibate, or if I need or want to be one.

"What do I do with my longings for intimacy? How do I live with my loneliness? Can I be happy and alone? What do I do when a woman invites me to be intimate with her? It is awfully tempting. Would it be so wrong to enter a relationship? Whom would I be hurting? Some of my colleagues think I'm crazy for not accepting such an invitation. But something in me says no. And if I say no, what do I do with my sexual feelings? Better yet, what do I do with my loneliness, with my love? Do I just numb them? I don't like numbing myself—it kills my spirit. What is the answer?"

This man did not choose celibacy; it was thrust upon him. He never planned on leading a single life, nor does he want to. Unlike the religious sister, he did not freely choose to live a celibate life, nor does he live in a community that supports and nourishes him. Unlike the divorced man, he did not choose to be single and does not engage in sexual affairs. More akin to the religious and laywoman than to the single man, this widower also wonders what he should do with his sexuality, with his yearning for intimacy, with his lonely love.

"Well, what do you do with sex if you want to remain celibate? Here I am: twenty-one, almost a college graduate, and still a virgin. I almost feel embarrassed, like I have to apologize because I haven't had sexual relations. I know that virginity is not the most popular thing on campus and that some consider me old-fashioned. But for whatever reason, I still think premarital sex is wrong for me. It may sound stupid, but I want to wait until marriage. It's a value I want to uphold. Sure, I admit I'd like to try it. Sometimes I get really horny and it's awfully tempting. Why do I feel one way and think another?

"Sure, guys and gals give me the argument that it all depends on the situation. You know—if two people are honest and sincere about their relationship and don't hurt anyone, then what's wrong with having sex? As long as you don't exploit another, sex is okay. They say it's a natural drive that should be satisfied. What am I, then—unnatural? I can't give them much of an argument. I can only say that since I wouldn't recommend premarital sex to my future kids, I wouldn't practice it myself."

Is this young woman puritanical, stupid, or out of touch with modern times? Must she feel embarrassed about her celibacy? If not, what can she do with her sexuality? What can she say to herself and others in support of a celibate life-style? How can she defend and proclaim her values?

Married woman: "I really think celibacy is a purer form of life. A celibate has fewer distractions and demands than a married person. Having no spouse and children can give you more freedom to do other things. Not only that, celibacy is 'purer' because it really puts the ability to live a meaningful life in your hands."

Celibate man: "I see what you mean and there's truth in what you say. But it's easy for you—a married person—to say that. You have a husband and children to support you. Think of going home to an empty house. There's no one there to say hello, no one to share the day's problems with. If a married person has a rough day, he or she can at least talk to someone. There's always someone at home to listen and help. I realize that married people have a lot of problems, and that I have considerable freedom as a celibate. Still, I'm alone."

Married woman: "Perhaps. I still say you have more opportunities; you have more time to do what you want. I know being alone can be painful, but it has benefits, too. Besides, married people are not always together. How do you think it feels to be alone and lonely when you're with someone? And there are times when I just want some rest and free time alone to do what I want to do, and it's almost impossible. Married people can feel alone, too, and they don't have the freedom you have."

Celibate man: "Don't forget sex. That's something I don't have, and it can solve a lot of problems."

Married woman: "What do you mean? Sex doesn't solve anything. If my husband and I are having problems, sex is the last thing I want. If sex solved problems, most people would be happy. If sex were only physical, I might agree with you. But sex is also emotional and spiritual. I can't separate sex and love. Having sex when there are problems only causes more problems."

Celibate man: "I'm not talking about physical sex. I agree that sex involves more than the physical. There should be some feeling or care. That's why I think a wife should always be available for her husband—because love means accepting what you don't like, and having sex even when you don't want to can heal a lot of hurt."

Married woman: "Just a minute, now. First of all, I don't like your chauvinistic attitude—that a wife should always be available to her husband. That's really old-fashioned. Isn't this a two-way street? Besides, I don't think you're right; it doesn't work that way. And what's wrong with hurting? Sometimes suffering pain is necessary to improve a marriage. For me, sex can be a way of running from problems, and consequently not helping either of us."

Celibate man: "Still, I think care, as little as it might be, can help. You have to admit that marriage is easier. You do have sex, and that beats loneliness. Sure, I can see that mere physical sex can be like masturbation, but it doesn't have to be that way."

Married woman: "No, I don't admit that marriage is easier. Once again, there's a lot of aloneness and loneliness in marriage, besides the many problems. To see sex as a panacea is a sexist and celibate fiction. Sex is only a part of marriage; it really can't go well unless the other parts are good, too."

Celibate man: "I agree that sex is only a part of life, but it can make a big difference. Sex usually involves more than sex. It's bound to draw you out of your lonely aloneness. Do you want to switch places?"

Married woman: "No, thank you. I chose to be married. Do you want to switch?"

Celibate man: "I don't know."

This married woman has chosen and is basically happy with her married life, but she feels that celibacy can be a meaningful alternative. She disagrees with some of the celibate's views on sex, which she judges to be sincere, though sexist, naive, and even magical. She enjoys sex but thinks that he overestimates its importance. She hints that marriage includes a celibate dimension and that other issues are more important than sex.

The celibate man, on the other hand, considers that celibacy and marriage have little in common. He values marriage over celibacy, but is uncertain if he would prefer to be married. He seems caught between sexual frustration and celibate freedom. Interestingly, this celibate regards sex as a healing power that can solve problems and alleviate loneliness.

Now let us consider the comments of some married people: "I am thirty-seven and I don't know what has happened to our marriage. It seems like a thousand years ago when we met; I was only fifteen when we seemed to be so much in love. We felt that everything was possible and nothing could stop us. Now, nothing seems possible. Where has our love gone?

"When we first married, we never wanted to separate. We couldn't stand being without each other. Now we are like strangers who happen to live at the same place. We can't or don't get close to each other. I thought I felt lonely before I got married; nothing beats this—being lonely and even alone when you're living with someone. When the kids were young, I didn't notice what was happening.

"I feel like I've always been taken for granted. I'm expected to do this, that, whatever, and no one seems to notice. Do they think everything gets done by magic? They don't realize how boring and demeaning my life can be. What would happen if I didn't cook? What would happen if I didn't slave for a day and a half to cook a Thanksgiving meal—a meal I have to schedule in between football games? To say the least, I'm angry.

"More important is that I—I— am taken for granted, expected to give, always be there, but receive little respect and appreciation in return. Sex is a fiasco. Strange, although I feel more sexual than ever before, we engage in sex much less frequently than before. We have sex when it fits my husband's schedule, which isn't very often. And sex with him is seldom very fulfilling. I end up more tense and frustrated. How do you think it feels to be lonelier after having sex? Sometimes I wonder if I'm worth anything to anyone. I'm tempted to try to find out."

This woman originally felt that marriage was the way to happiness. Now she feels empty, harried, lonely, and alone. She feels like a function rather than a person. Love is absent. Her spirit is exhausted and starved. She feels exploited, as one used to satisfy the needs of others. She wants appreciation, concern, love. She wonders if she might find it elsewhere.

"I am frustrated, angry, and fed up with sex. After twelve years of marriage, you would think my husband and I would be closer. Instead, we seem farther apart. We seem only to function with each other. We have become friendly strangers.

"His obtuseness amazes me. He doesn't even understand why I refuse to go to bed with him; it's because we rarely share otherwise. This may appear selfish, but I want to be Number One, not a poor second to work, newspaper, television, and golf. Is this too much to ask? When he does try to share himself—which is rare—he's so hesitant and inept. What is he afraid of? I'm not going to kill him.

"I feel like a service station where people stop to refuel and then drive away; I give and give, but get little appreciation and love in return. My husband says he loves me, but he seldom shows it. He doesn't seem to understand what I want. He says that he's satisfied; he can't understand why I have so many complaints. Sometimes I doubt myself. But no; I know I'm right.

"It's not easy to live with someone who is in his own world—a world he seldom shares. It hurts a lot to live with someone and yet to be very, very lonely. Sure, I enjoy sex very much, but I'm not going to give myself in the bedroom if my husband doesn't share in the family room. I can't understand how he does it. I feel used. I only want consistent affection and sharing. Is that asking for too much?"

This woman, too, reflects the feelings and concerns of many women. She feels taken for granted, frustrated, and angry. She experiences a violation of her dignity and integrity if she engages in genital sex without loving in other ways as well. She wants to be the center of her husband's concern, to be shown love consistently and concretely—as she has shown for him. Also, her spirit is undernourished.

"I hate to admit it, but I'm terribly scared of being impotent. That's one problem I never thought I'd have. I simply can't perform the way I used to. And worse yet, I seldom have the desire for sex. And look, I'm not old yet; I'm forty-four. Or am I? I always feel so tired; there's always something else to do.

"I get the feeling my wife expects more of me and is disappointed in me. God, how I hate to go on vacations alone with her. I don't know what to do with her. I wonder how she feels about it. I guess we should talk.

"Why do I kid myself? We haven't really talked much for years. I wouldn't know what to say. I'd feel so afraid and helpless. Yet, something should be done. Marriage has to be more than a tense adjustment, a keeping out of each other's way. I really try, but my efforts seem so inadequate. Hell, I was happier when I was single. I was by myself—and sure, I felt lonely, but I wasn't so miserable and alone."

This man wants intimacy but is afraid of it. He wants to communicate, but does not know how; he feels vulnerable. He tells of being anxious about sexual inadequacy. He dreads what he wants most: love. Uncomfortable as a married single who merely adjusts to living with someone, he wonders if being an unmarried single would be better than his marital charades. Like the woman, his spirit suffers.

Here is another man's story: "Honestly, I really do try, but it seems I'm not good enough. After twenty-six years of marriage, my wife complains more than ever. Her main criticism is that I don't share my feelings, that I don't say what I think and feel. But when I do try to share, she criticizes me for being wrong or unfair. Then, of course, I withdraw. Wouldn't you?

"Besides, men aren't taught to share; in fact, it's often the opposite. I don't mean to use this as an excuse, but it's true. It's not just male society and mass media, but women also have a part in it. You know, most males are highly influenced by their mothers—women. And I know that my dad was not the best role model in this respect. Why can't women help instead of criticizing?

"Why do women always have to bring up things from the past? Good grief! My wife talks intensely about things that happened twenty years ago. It seems she has to have everything resolved; otherwise she can't be at ease. We must talk before we have a good time. Why can't she just let the past be in the past, or at least put it on the shelf for awhile? I'm sick and tired of talking things out—just burned out; give me a break."

This man echoes the thoughts and feelings of many men. He perceives himself as trapped between pressure to share and criticism for not meeting his wife's expectations. Besides being frustrated, he is confused and angry about his wife's (woman's?) and his (man's?) approaches. His spirit, too, is drained.

All marriages are not sad. Consider this man's experience. "After thirty-five years of marriage, I can say that my wife and I love each other and enjoy living together more than ever. I respect and trust my wife, believe in her, and like her. I am grateful that she puts up with a bozo like me, but she says the same about herself. I guess we are two funny people in love. That's good to say, but when I tell people I am happily married, they look at me as if I'm giving them a line.

"Oh yes, we have had our rough times—with each other and with the kids. But somehow we grew stronger through those difficult times. I couldn't see this when it was happening, but in looking back I can see we are both better and stronger persons now. But we worked on it. Speaking for myself, I found it difficult learning to share my feelings and to take the time to listen. I think I'm a better man for it.

"Sex? It's better than ever. How about that! We don't do it as often as when we were young, but our relationship both in and out of sex is more fulfilling and satisfying. We are closer. Since the kids are out of the house, we have more opportunity just to be with each other. It's almost like when we were first married, only better."

Single and celibate persons also can have happy and successful lives that include being sexually vital and integrated. Consider this single woman's reflections: "I am a single, sixty-four-year-old woman who many today would consider to be something of an anomaly. Let me explain.

"Through hard work and good fortune I have become a successful teacher, lecturer, and writer. More importantly, I am happy being single. While in school many years ago, I seldom gave married, single, or religious life much serious thought. After graduate school, I became more open to what might occur. Only in my early thirties did I begin to think seriously about which life or vocation would be best for me. I eventually chose a road less traveled—the single life—and I think it is the best life for me. From a faith perspective, I feel that God called, and is still calling me, to be single because it is the best way for me to realize myself most fully. I am convinced that being single rather than a religious or married person has offered me the optimum opportunities to live a life of love—to love myself, others, and God.

"It's good now to feel that I didn't miss the boat—that I got on and stayed on the right boat for me. Many people believe they missed the boat, regretting missed opportunities or wrong choices in their personal and professional lives. I have no regrets; I can honestly say I'd do it again, and in essentially the same way. Of course, life has not been perfect; I've had my share of suffering. But the single life has been my way to grow and become more perfect.

"I know that some people feel sorry for me because I never married or got sexually involved with a man. They have had difficulty understanding and appreciating how I could be single and happy. They shouldn't be sorry for me; I believe I'm happier and more fulfilled than most people, married or single. There are also those confused by my vitality and serenity. I seem to threaten them. Many can't believe I would rather be single than married. I am not an Old Maid—a sexless, spiritless prune. Although my body is aging, I still feel vital, sexual, enthusiastic, and creative. I'm more fully alive than ever.

"Sure, I have been lonely at times through the years, but it has never lasted long. I saw these times as opportunities to reflect on my life, especially my relationships with my family, friends, and God. I think loneliness actually helped me to appreciate and love them better. I refused to feel sorry for myself; I never placed my well-being in another's hands. My loneliness motivated me to depend only on God and to be self-sufficient.

"Of course I felt very sexual at times—and I still do. I understand this as a natural affirmation of my womanhood and of my desire to be intimate with a man. I accept my sexual feelings as positive forces; I do not fight them. I sublimate them in physical and social activities. I have learned also to suppress and detach from them. Most of all, I avoid sexualizing myself, i.e., identifying myself with my sexuality. Instead, I enjoy my sexuality along with the other precious parts of my personality. When I isolate my sexuality from the whole, I feel myself getting into trouble. Believe it or not, I am glad I have lived a celibate life—and I do not consider myself less sexual than my married or genitally active sisters and brothers. See, I warned you that I listen to a different drum."

The foregoing married and unmarried people represent some of the concerns raised by human sexuality. Differences between men and women, different ways of living one's sexuality emerge in these and other experiences. The chapters that follow will offer ways to live healthier and holier sexual lives. Single, celibate, and marital living will be presented as distinct life-forms which call for both similar and different modes of sexual behavior. Contrary to popular opinion, celibacy and/or singlehood do not mean being nonsexual or asexual, but rather being sexual in a way that differs from marital sexuality. Ideally, vowed celibate and single persons can and should be sexual in all ways except the way of genital gratification. Married persons can and should be celibate with all people except with their spouses. In whatever way we choose to shape our life and direct our sexuality, we shall see that we have common ground in our search for intimacy and a spiritual dimension.

CHAPTER 2

Being a Sexual Person

What constitutes healthy human sexuality? The answer to this varies according to our assumptions about personality, sexuality, and health. These assumptions influence the way we think and feel about, judge and act on our sexuality. For instance, those who hold that sex is merely physical, that one sex is superior to the other, that our behavior has no effect on others, or that celibates are not sexual, will have a different experience of sexuality than those who believe sex is wholistic, that males and females are equal and complementary, that our actions have an impact on others, and that celibates are sexual persons.

Let us consider what it means to be sexual, human, and healthy. This will give us the framework for understanding the various modes of sexuality and their corresponding healthy and nonhealthy experiences.

Sex and sexuality

Sex refers to the conditions of embodiment that predispose and co-determine how we relate to objects, events, and persons. As its etymology indicates (from Latin *secare*, to cut), sex is relational. Our sex, primarily male-female or female-male, highly influences the way we experience reality. Thus, being primarily a man or a woman—which is due to both nature (sex) and nurture (gender)—co-forms the way we interact with one another and other realities as well.

Because we are *embodied* selves, we are sexual. This is not to say that anatomy determines our destiny, but rather that our embodiment co-constitutes our way of being sexual. Instead of focusing on biology, physiology, or any kind of perspective or study of experience, the emphasis is on our lived sexual body—

on what our sexuality means in experience.

Sexual embodiment means that we manifest ourselves and relate to one another in a sexual way—primarily as a man or a woman. I am my body/sexuality, and my body/sexuality is me. When someone looks at or comments on my body, they look at or comment on me, on my person. When someone treats me as a sex object or just a body, they insult and degrade me. When my body changes, I change. My body/sexuality is not something I simply have or possess, but is an essential part of who and what I am. Embodiment is primarily a mode of being. These statements may sound simple or complex, but they can be forgotten in daily living. We can forget that we *are* sexually embodied people.

Many Western thinkers and teachers have taught that the body is secondary, that the soul, spirit, psyche, or mind is what is really human or primary. They have reasoned that our bodies are mere containers for the "deeper" realities. Although we may want to embrace the truth, "We are our bodies," many attitudes and expressions betray a tendency to see our bodies as things we possess to contain the spirit, as objects to observe, to use, or to treat. Scientists, biologists, and physicians, although helping us in important ways, have reinforced this tendency. When we view ourselves—our (sexual) bodies—as secondary or as objects, we find it hard to express, to appreciate, to enjoy, and to celebrate our (sexual) bodies/selves.

For instance, a woman's menstrual process is not simply a physiological fact; it is an experiential phenomenon. Although increasingly more women (and some men) are aware of the biochemical impact of menstruation, the menstrual cycle is primarily experiential. Since a woman has and is her body, her menstrual cycle influences the way she experiences reality. Many women, for instance, experience a cyclic change in mood and attitude. This is not to say that a woman is determined by her menstrual cycle; she can choose her attitude and response to this experiential phenomenon. Emphatically, the menstrual process is a bodily experience that women simply do not have as if they possess a thing; it is an experience that they are.

Embodiment means that a person's sociality is in some way sexual. Embodiment makes us humanly manifest—accessible and available to others—as men or as women. To see, hear, touch, yearn for, think about, speak to, or relate in whatever way to another is an embodiment, and therefore a sexual act. We will see later that since we are essentially social beings, sexuality is never exclusively a private affair. Sexuality is a social reality, and sociality is sexual.

Embodiment (being incarnated) also means that our sexuality is psychological and spiritual. Psychologically, our knowledge of, attitude toward, and ways we cope with sexuality significantly influence our experience of and degree of healthy or nonhealthy sexuality. Sexuality is also spiritual: sexuality embodies, explicitly or implicitly, the spiritual dimension.

Technically, "sex" can indicate a relatively static dimension of personhood, confined to the conditions which define the differentiations of the sexes. Sex can refer to our inheritance which gives us the possibility and necessity of being sexual. Nature, however, is meaningless without nurture, and potentially is static without learning. How our sex is actualized is contingent on both inheritance and environment. The actualization of sex can be called sexuality. We experience sex, have sex, make sex, express sex, cope with sex, use sex, enjoy sex, celebrate sex, are sexual. Sexuality, in contrast to sex, points to a more dynamic aspect of personhood: to the interaction of sex and gender. Thus, sexuality or how we are sexual is contingent on sex and just as much or more on how we learn to be male and female.

Femininity and masculinity are parts of sexuality. Consider femininity as the way a woman has learned to manifest her sex, or how a woman has learned certain sex roles within a particular culture. Femininity represents *learned* and sanctioned ways of being a woman. For instance, being feminine is associated in most cultures with the qualities of sensitivity, intuition, receptivity, emotionality, nourishment, and care. Likewise, masculinity is a mode of sexuality that a man *learns* in a particular culture. Being masculine usually connotes that a man learns certain social ways to be sexual. In the United States and elsewhere this is expressed in the qualities of objectivity, logic, activity, competition, rationality, and task-oriented behavior. Although emphasis is placed on cultural learning, masculinity and femininity also include sex and/or inherited factors—for instance, genetics, biochemistry, physiology, the brain, and so on influence masculinity and femininity. We will see, however, that a woman must incorporate so-called masculine qualities and a man must realize so-called feminine qualities in order to be healthy.

Thus, being male or female—being sexual—is considered to be a function of both inheritance and learning. How a person is sexual is determined by his or her inheritance, by the environment and society/culture, and by the person's attitude. Again, we emphasize that sexuality is not merely a biological entity, but rather the way a person embodies (manifests and relates to) his or her physical, psychosocial, spiritual, and aesthetic self.

In light of clinical and empirical evidence, both men and women are considered to be androgynous: within every man there is a woman, and within every woman there is a man. Although the sexes are distinct, they are not separate. A phenomenology of sexual experience indicates that a man and a woman experience something similar and something foreign in each other, and that one sex is the challenging complement of the other sex. In Jungian terms, a man encounters and/or projects his *anima* and a woman her *animus* upon the other sex. Ideally, each sex should complement the other—men and women helping each other rather than one dominating the other. Such complementary growth is possible because all people are androgynous.

Thus, sex and sexuality are matters of accent, the accent being on male or female. Being a woman means that a person is a member of the female sex that incorporates male sexuality. It can be said that a woman's femaleness is primarily in the foreground and her maleness in the background. Likewise, being a man means that a person belongs to the male sex which incorporates female sexuality. The *anima* and *animus* are biological, psychological, social, cultural, and spiritual forces.

Later on we will describe and analyze three distinct and interrelated modes of sexuality: primary, affective, and genital sexuality. A common and frequently male mistake is to genitalize sexuality, forgetting or minimizing the other modes of sexuality. Although genital sexuality is part of being a sexual person, genitality does not define sexuality. Feminists have correctly focused on and demonstrated the importance of a more basic type of sexuality—that of being a sexual person, male or female. Our discussion will include male and female sexuality, genital and primary sexuality, and a third type known as affective sexuality. Furthermore, each of these modes of sexuality will be analyzed from a physical, functional, aesthetic, and spiritual perspective.

Dimensions of human personhood

Our experience of sexuality and the meaning we give it depends on our understanding of the structure and dynamics of human personhood. All of us hold assumptions about the nature and the nurture of full and ethical humanity. We have a philosophical anthropology that comes from inheritance, childrearing, mass media, culture, education, and so on. These preconscious theories of personality highly influence the way we look at, judge, and deal with ourselves and others.

For example, an approach to sexuality that excludes the spiritual dimension will give sexual experiences a meaning radically different from one that includes the spiritual: premarital and extramarital genital sex is easily justified when the spiritual is excluded; including the spiritual makes the experience and meaning of such sexual behavior significantly different. Likewise, if the physical and/or psychosocial dimensions are excluded or minimized, the meaning of sexuality is fragmented.

Human beings experience reality in four fundamental ways and combinations thereof: physically, functionally, spiritually, and aesthetically. We will use these modes of existence and motivational systems in our analyses of sexuality.

The *physical* dimension of a person refers to the structure and dynamics of a person's embodied-incarnated self. Though none of us is ever exclusively physical, we act in certain ways when we invest most of our energy in our pre-rational, physical self. The body demands immediate satisfaction—pleasure, comfort, a reduction of tension and/or pain. When we experience urgent bodily need, we cannot wait; postponement of satisfaction makes little sense. We are "a needy me" and are prone to act impulsively, without thinking of consequences to self or others. When we try to exist in an exclusively physical way, we want our needs satisfied regardless of anything or anybody.

For instance, an infant is a bodily self who craves immediate satisfaction no matter what. Infants are narcissistic; life is centered around them. When an adult acts in this way, he or she manifests regressive behavior: an adult desperately in need of food may lose all respect for self and others and act impulsively to gain immediate satisfaction.

The physical mode of sexuality directs us to act almost exclusively on the physical level; some of our energy will be invested in physical sexual gratification. When engaging in such physical sex, we can easily lose respect for self and others. If we maximize the physical dimension of sex, we see others and ourselves simply as sex objects to be used.

The *functional* dimension refers to ego activities centered around task-oriented behavior, coping mechanisms, and cognitive-rational activities. Functionality describes how we function—the means we take to achieve our goals. As human beings, this involves coping rationally with situations; we analyze a situation and decide how to act. Most of us can rationally deal with our internal feelings and thoughts and with environmental demands.

Functioning normally involves coping and adjusting, maintaining ourselves, and having adequate control of our lives. When we invest energy in our functional powers, we can usually operate successfully. A danger, however, is to be so objective and task-oriented that we lack affective sensitivity, intimacy, and spiritual sensibility. We can live from the neck up—and "be" out of our minds.

Information and analysis of sexuality can help to improve sexuality, but theory and technique should primarily serve experience; otherwise, we apply techniques for achieving sexual satisfaction, but seldom give, receive, and let go for any extended period of time. Objective control can impede spontaneity, love, and transcendence—essential qualities of healthy sexual relations. Excessively rational attitudes can lead to exploitation and manipulation.

The *spiritual* dimension as discussed here does not explicitly include theology or sacred Scripture; it is phenomenological. However, "supernatural" or other sources are not denied or judged meaningless; our approach is congruent with these and other perspectives.

From a functional ego perspective, we deal with life as an unending series of problems to reflect on and solve; spiritually, we encounter life as a perpetual mystery to suffer and celebrate. Both processes are necessary for healthy living. The spiritual, however, is paramount because it is transcendent.

Transcendence does not suggest that we go out of this world; rather, we go deeper into the world where we experience the unity of objects, events, and persons. Such spiritual experiences as compassion, wonder, contemplation, and love are neither irrational nor rational; they are transrational. The experience of transcendence involves appreciating and responding to the way individual parts of reality are interrelated to form a whole. Clinically, this means all human beings are radically interconnected with one another, that our primary state is to be in community. Individuality is important and essential, but it is secondary to community. Stated ethically, this implies that whatever we do has impact on others.

Spiritual experiences involve paradox, mystery, and transcendence. Unlike the "either-or" process of the functional ego, spiritual dynamics are an experience of "both-and." Instead of dealing with clear and distinct ideas, spiritual selves revere and surrender to mystery—a clearly unclear and inexhaustibly accessible source of meaning and fulfillment.

Healthy spiritual sex incorporates qualities and activities such as care, respect, gentleness and, most importantly, love. Spirit deepens sex, and sex embodies spirit. Sexuality gives spirituality concrete humanness; spirituality gives sexuality lasting vitality. We will see that in spiritual genital sexuality a person can experience an aesthetic unity of concrete sexuality and transcendent spirituality. Indeed, healthy spirituality can never be sexless because spirituality is always in some way embodied. Likewise, sexuality is always more or less spiritual because it is inclined toward transcendence—a going beyond individuality toward communion with others and God.

Too often, however, spirituality and sexuality are separated. We can try to repress and violate the transcendent—the urge for communion—in our sexuality, but even these attempts are affirmations of the spiritual. Or instead of despiritualizing sexuality, we can desexualize spirituality: some well-intentioned people strive to live spiritual lives by repressing their sexuality, especially genital sexuality, or they consider genital sexuality as only a biological function, consequently degrading human personhood. To repress sexuality while promoting spirituality is similar to repressing spirituality while promoting sexuality; both are unchaste. One approach identifies the human person simply as a rational spiritual being; the other approach makes the human person simply a sexual rational being. In fact, the human person is a unity of physicality, functionality, and spirituality.

The *aesthetic* dimension refers to the unity of the physical, rational, and spiritual. For example, art is a harmony of matter, technique, and transcendent meaning—that is, it is embodied, rational, and spiritual. When we say that a woman is beautiful, we do not necessarily mean that she is physically pretty or attractive, but that she lives in harmony, manifesting (embodiment) transcendent meaning (spirituality) with good form (functionality). When we repress or dissociate any of these three dimensions, we become less beautiful and more or less "mad" and "sad."

Aesthetic sex protects and promotes the unity of matter, technique, and spiritual meaning. The beauty of sex is experienced; beauty is seen as sexual. Most spiritual (loving) sex is beautiful because it is embodied, has form or style, and incorporates love or spiritual meaning. We are challenged to seek beautiful and transcendent sex: to experience the union of self and others, to go out of ourselves to and for each other, to experience the presence of God.

Healthy, good, normal, mad, and bad sexuality

We have seen that any mode of sexuality—primary, genital, or affective—can be dominantly physical, functional, spiritual, or aesthetic. Before we begin to focus our study of sexuality, we should clarify a few more variables in our framework; namely, healthy, good, normal, mad, and bad sexuality.

Healthy sexuality is congruent with and fosters wholistic growth. Instead of living out of repression, fixation, regression, perversion, disintegration, or any psychopathology, healthy persons grow in wholeness and promote the welfare of self and others. The essential dynamic in healthy sex is committed love without psychopathology and immaturity. Healthy sex is good and beautiful because it promotes the appreciation and nourishment of our physicality, functionality, and spirituality.

Madness characterizes those who are closed to experiences significant to and necessary for wholistic growth. Normal people—not just abnormal people—can alienate themselves from experiences vital to healthy and happy living, and therefore be "mad." In normal madness, we function within the confines of normal society and do not manifest pathological symptoms;

nonetheless, we are closed to realities necessary for healthy living. For instance, workaholics—their ultimate concern is work or task-oriented success. They minimize other essential experiences such as love, play, and compassion. Workaholics, consequently, are normal but more or less mad because they live less than wholistic lives. We will see that many kinds of sexual activity are not unhealthy but are nevertheless normal and more or less mad. An example is genital activity that only reduces tension but does not promote individual and communal growth. It may be normal and mad, neither unhealthy nor healthy.

Mad sex usually lacks such qualities as awareness, care, responsibility, respect, and love. Some mad sex is psychologically unhealthy (e.g., sexual perversions and offenses); other sexual behavior, though not judged to be abnormally mad or socially punishable, is normally mad. For instance, treating another person as a sex object is normal and mad because it violates the whole person, especially the spirituality of sexuality that urges one to move closer to union with others and God.

Sexual behavior can also be considered in light of goodness and badness. In the psychospiritual framework we are using, *goodness* refers to behavior that is congruent with and fosters healthy love, to behavior that promotes the welfare of community: self, others, and God. *Badness* refers to the violation or destruction of communal growth and welfare. We can see that goodness/badness and healthy/nonhealthy can be related but are distinct and can be quite different. For instance, we can be unhealthy but good: neurotic or psychotic persons do not have to be bad for they may conscientiously try to promote love and growth of self and others and try to respond to God's presence. Other sick persons, however, may intentionally and consistently violate life and live contrary to love. On the other hand, normal persons who are not unhealthy in the traditional sense can be bad. Although these people are well adjusted and lack pathology, they fail to live according to the spiritual dictum of love.

The fundamental difference between being mad and being bad is the individual's level of intentionality. Mad persons seldom consciously or intentionally promote madness; usually unconscious or organic processes motivate them. In contrast to mad people, bad people are more intentional and exercise more choices in doing what they do. Nevertheless, mad persons can choose to be bad. Indeed, all of us are sometimes more or less mad and/or bad. The degree of our madness and badness reflects our lack of healthiness and/or holiness.

Truly healthy persons are at least implicitly good because they promote communal wholeness and growth. To be sure, healthy persons are capable of and can perform bad acts, but basically their lives are good: their paramount value is to live a life of love. Normal persons who lead consistently good (loving) lives are healthy.

Healthy sexuality includes an integration of the sexual and the spiritual. Sexuality focuses on embodiment and spirituality accents love. Sexuality can vitalize, concretize, and incarnate the spiritual; spirituality can nourish, deepen, and transcend sexuality. But when we bifurcate sexuality and spirituality, we identify ourselves and others simply as sexual or spiritual beings, and therefore are unwholly (mad) people. Although mere physical sex may incorporate pleasurable satisfaction and temporary fulfillment, such sex has little joy, depth, and permanency because it represses its spiritual force and robs us of what we can be. Love (spirit) without sex becomes disembodied, dry, lifeless, and mad. Sexless people become either cerebral robots or untouchable spirits.

The ideal is to experience, not simply talk about, the lived unity of spirituality and sexuality. The challenge is to embody and manifest love in sex, which is both a sexual and spiritual task. Healthy and holy people witness to this unity of sexuality and spirituality.

In the next three chapters, we will describe and analyze primary, affective, and genital sexuality in their physical, functional, spiritual, and aesthetic dimensions. We will show how they can be healthy, good, mad, or bad. When physicality, functionality, and spirituality are integrated, sexuality is good, beautiful, healthy, and holy.

CHAPTER 3

Primary Sexuality

Do men and women interpret, cope with, and experience life differently? Are we or should we be the same? Empirical and clinical data show that men and women differ not only biologically but also psychosocially and spiritually. However, this does not imply that one sex is superior to the other; it means that the sexes are different, equal, and complementary. How and why are men and women different and similar? How can we challenge and help each other to be better men and women and to live in harmony?

Primary sexuality is one model that accounts for an individual's mode of sexual existence—how he or she is present to and interacts with him/herself, others, to reality in general, and to God. It asserts that each person has an inherent propensity to be primarily a man or a woman. This should not be understood as biological or structural determinism; rather, it merely states that structural conditions of the human person serve as the infrastructure or framework for any environmental learning. Instead of being mutually exclusive, heredity and environment are interdependent. While focusing on the nature and nurture of men and women, the following propositions shed light on sexual differences, similarities, and complementarities. They are not offered as absolute explanations of the sexes; they are used heuristically to clarify and integrate much of the data from both the heredity and environmental approaches to sexuality.

Male and female existence

Based on phenomenological and other research, one proposition is that women tend to interweave their experience and men tend to differentiate their experience. Due to innate and environmental focuses, women tend relatively more toward wholeness, internalization, and concrete care, while men tend toward categorization, externalization, and abstract principles. Women's experiences are prone more than men's to seek an integral and centralized process, while men's experiences are more prone to be compartmentalized. A woman experiences reality as a network of many factors (objects, events, and persons) that she cares for; a man copes with the individual parts of reality. To be sure, these propensities are not mutually exclusive. Because we are (by nature and nurture) androgynous, we can and do, more or less, actualize both sexual possibilities. The challenge for us is to realize both while remaining true to our primary sexual identity.

Consider the case of a wife and husband who have been tense and aggressive toward each other throughout the day and have not reconciled. The woman will usually be less inclined than the man to be intimate that particular night. The man, however, can usually differentiate his experiences more easily; in this case, the troublesome day and the intimate encounter. A woman is not inclined to compartmentalize her experiences. When the husband expects his wife to put the day aside and make love, she likely will look at him as if he is out of his mind and think, "How can he even consider being intimate when the day has been so miserable? Does he think I can push a button to turn the day off? If we can't make love outside the bedroom, we're not going to make it inside the bedroom. What does he think I am—a robot?" The husband thinks, "What the hell's wrong with her? So we had a rough day—does that mean we shouldn't have sex? Why can't she just forget about the day and have some fun at night?"

The perception and judgment of both the husband and the wife have assets and deficits (although I favor the woman's sensibility). The woman is right: genital intimacy is not something one disassociates from the rest of the day; intimacy should be integrated with and be the culmination of an ongoing intimacy. Sexual intimacy without other forms of intimacy can become exploitive and phony—a kind of prostitution. Sexual activity can easily serve as a cover and anesthetic for underlying problems.

However, the man's sensibility is not meaningless: to suppress or to put things on the shelf for awhile can engender reconciliation as well as an enjoyable time. If every problem had to be worked out before intimacy could occur, intimacy would be greatly curtailed. Nevertheless, to frequently minimize or repress problems will sooner or later harm sexual intimacy and perhaps destroy the overall relationship.

Women more often than men will seek to unify sex and love. For instance, when a woman is inclined toward genital involvement with a man, she usually seeks a sign of love. Although such a request may be linked to a need for approval, a woman's integrative propensity encourages her to look for love in sex. To be sure, a woman can separate sex and love, but a man usually separates them more readily. Similarly, although a woman can be intimately involved with more than one man at a time, she rarely engages in such multi-involvement. A man, however, can live separate lives more easily. A "family man"—an apparently good husband and father—can yet periodically engage a prostitute or have an affair. A woman can also seek promiscuous activity, but she is less likely to do so not only because of social factors but because of her primary sexuality.

Men's differentiated mode of existence explains their tendency to put various experiences in different categories. They involve themselves in one experience while putting others aside. Their task-oriented manner can pressure them, though not necessarily, to be more detached from and less intimate with their experience. Indulging in genital sex without love or ongoing emotional attachment is easier for them than for women.

Moreover, men can be sexually involved with more than one woman. It is as if they can put women in separate categories. Leaving one woman, a man can put her aside and later be intimate with another—sometimes in a seemingly genuine way. A woman, on the other hand, has more difficulty in romancing more than one "number one." The two or more men would, it seems, conflict within her personality. Of course, one sex is capable of doing what the other can do. Our intent here, however, is to describe the dynamics of what usually happens.

Again, consider how a man can treat a woman as a sex object—almost exclusively in physical terms. He can dissociate her physical sexuality from the rest of her being, fragmenting the whole woman and concentrating on her physical attributes. Indeed, a woman also can see and treat a man as a sex object, but not quite as easily or as often. She is inclined, sooner than later, to look for more than one dimension of a man.

Since all people are androgynous, women can differentiate experiences and be task-oriented; men can interweave experiences and be caring. In this sense, a man should strive to be more like a woman, and a woman to be more like a man, while retaining the ideal of complementarity. A man should learn to appreciate in himself and in women how the parts of experience impact on one another, and to care for (not just deal with) others. He should seek to promote and actualize the anima within himself. A woman should learn to differentiate her experiences—to realize the animus within her.

Cultural programming and personal expectations notwithstanding, women's integrative, caring style and men's differentiated, task-oriented style may influence their choice of and performance in a career and/or jobs (as well as parenting). A female physician, for example, may see and care for patients a little differently than a male physician. Also, patients may experience the female and male physician differently. This is not to imply that one gender of physician is better than the other, but rather that a physician of one gender may be better than another for a particular individual. Given a male and a female gynecologist of equal competence, some women would prefer the one to the other not only because of personal and professional competence but also because of the way the male or female physician interacts with and treats the patient by virtue of their primary sexuality.

Another example is male and female architects. A female architect might design a building (particularly for women) differently than a man. Perceiving reality and women from the perspective of a woman may influence her to conceive a dwelling place that would differ from what a man would conceive. Her architectural vision may be influenced by her primary sexuality. Remember, a man is capable of realizing his femaleness, and a woman her maleness. Nevertheless, it is possible to have architecture (or anything else) that is primarily male or female. And it is possible that our U.S. architecture as well as other things are one-sidedly male.

Let's probe this example further. A woman's dwelling place may be more important to her. If so, the architecture, furnishings, art works, general structure, and atmosphere of her home would be congruent with and promote her female experience. Unfortunately, men usually have designed and imposed on women living conditions that are less than optimum for a woman's comfort and development. Female community structures such as convents and dormitories (as well as working areas) are often more linear, staid, functional, and "masculine" rather than centered, dynamic, caring, and "feminine." A woman may be more intimately involved with her space; her place may be an important expression of herself. A man, on the other hand, may be more detached from his space or may focus on its utility. Again, these tendencies are not mutually exclusive.

Time also may be experienced differently. A woman may tend to interweave the past and future with the present, whereas a man may be prone to separate them. Thus, when dealing with a present issue, a woman may be more likely to bring up past events as well as future possibilities. The man more commonly wants to deal with the issue at hand and may become irritated with evoking the past or the implications for the future. He wants to solve the problem and "forget" about it. In time, one approach without the other will become one-sided and increasingly stressful.

Neither the male nor female mode of existence is superior; both are equal and essential. One without the other leads to a fragmented and impoverished life and culture. Men need to realize their female and feminine dimensions in their male and masculine ways, and women need to realize their male and masculine dimensions in their female and feminine ways. They become whole but not the same, alike but not identical. Such an androgynous integration of both male-masculine and female-feminine presence is needed for healthy living. To clarify and expand these ideas more concretely, let us consider the experience of primary sexuality from four perspectives: the physical, functional, spiritual, and aesthetic.

The experience of primary sexuality

Reflect on primary sexuality in its *physical* dimension. For instance, if we judge our body or sex as inferior, we can feel and act inferior. We can be programmed to feel that our bodies include certain meanings and exclude others. For instance, a woman may see her sexuality primarily as a means for childbearing, pleasing men, and being useful to men. She can learn to experience her sexuality exclusively as an instrument used by other people, especially children and men. Or a woman may be programmed to view her sexuality as an ornament to attract and generate male applause. To be concerned about personal appearance is healthy, but when it is a compulsion, then fixation, docility, self-minimization, resentment, and unhappiness are likely consequences. Most mass media and advertisements reinforce this sexist madness.

Men, also, can be conditioned to have negative attitudes toward their sexuality. A man, for instance, may have a body image that stresses superiority over women. A man with a small body may feel inferior because Western culture promotes a large and powerful ideal of the male body. Men, however, retain social acceptance when their bodies get out of shape, while women can be pressured to stay "attractive" and "in shape" when in public or on display. An overweight woman may encounter more obstacles to job promotions and marital prospects than a man will experience.

When we treat one another as sex objects, we focus exclusively on the other's body as if that person is simply "a body" or some being that has a body—"somebody." This is evidence of a lack of respect for the whole person; it is an insult to that person. A person treated as a sex object feels degraded and often resentful. Instead of being appreciated as a whole person, this person is fragmented by being perceived simply as a body to be exploited. The truth is that there is no such entity as "a body" but only a psychospiritual body or an embodied spirit. Making a person a thing excludes or at least minimizes the person's functional, aesthetic, and spiritual dimensions; the person is dehumanized. Such an attitude is not true to reality and is less than healthy.

Turning to primary sexuality in its *functional* dimension, it is important to consider not so much what men and women do but how they do it. We have seen that both men and women can care and be task-oriented, but how they implement these activities differs. A househusband's experience of and the way he functions with children and housework may differ from a housewife's experience. A female physician can do a job as well as or better than a man, but how she interacts with her patients and how they experience her differs from that of a male physician.

With the exception of certain biological processes, few activities are exclusively male or female in themselves. Both men and women can and should have the opportunity to function in any area. Ideally, both sexes should do many of the same activities in complementary ways. Injustice and problems occur when one sex acts superior, oppresses the other sex to compensate for underlying inferiority, or strives to be the same as the other sex.

Women have been and are oppressed in career (functional) areas. Instead of being hindered from pursuing certain fields, women should be encouraged to be slightly different engineers, physicians, or mechanics than men. This difference would not be due entirely to cultural programming. A woman's caring and centering posture can engender a service distinct from a man's more detached and differentiated disposition. Both modes of functioning are equal and complementary.

Social programming, however, can militate against the growth of complementary, androgynous service. For instance, women can be seen as inferior, compliant, and too emotional. They may learn to think of themselves in this way. Consequently, possibilities for personal and professional fulfillment are excluded. Such oppression can begin in early childhood. Consider children's books: little boys who grow up to be men are often the center of the story whereas little girls who grow up to be women are on the fringe of the action, waiting to serve. How often is a physician, an engineer, a mechanic, or a minister depicted as a woman? Even if girls are depicted in traditionally male roles, what are their chances of pursuing these fields in real life? These and many other kinds of cultural conditioning can impede primary sexual functioning.

It is important to remember that being a little girl sets the foundation for being a woman and that being a little boy is the groundwork from which a man grows. People, especially parents, positively and negatively influence what kind of woman or man a person will be and how he or she will function. If a woman as a girl could play only in "feminine" ways, her view of being a woman was already being formed to a large degree. If she were allowed to be assertive, to stand up for her rights, and to do so-called "masculine" things, she probably would grow up with a different view of being a woman and would, consequently, function differently.

Since a woman's cultural and subcultural programming highly

influences her self-concept and sexual roles, a woman should ask herself certain questions: Did (or does) my mother sell herself short, act like a servant, or take second place to men? Does she take pride in who she is, enjoy doing many things, feel equal to men, and feel free? What is her view of womanhood? Did (and does) she think that women are just as important and contribute as much as men? Did she encourage me to be competent and competitive as well as caring and receptive? How did my father act toward me and my mother? Did (and does) he treat me delicately and discourage me from culturally defined male activities? Or did he encourage me to function as well as and to succeed as much as boys? How do my parents treat me now?

A girl may undergo pressures that boys seldom experience. Although some girls may have the freedom in childhood to be an individual and to be aggressive, they can be pressured in adolescence to subordinate their vocational goals to the finding of a marital partner. Instead of being encouraged to seek autonomous self-esteem contingent on self-worth and ability, female adolescents are often pressured to feel that their self-esteem primarily depends on how well they please and are affirmed by men. Indeed, attitudes are changing under the influence of women's studies and feminist movements. Still, one need only observe mass media to see the enormous amount of sexism against both sexes.

Although much focus today is on women's rights, men also have been oppressed and impeded from becoming wholly themselves, perhaps as much or more so than women. Many men have been culturally programmed to distrust their feelings of affection and/or fail to learn how to be intimate. Cognition and task-oriented behavior are emphasized. Their self-esteem often depends too much on career success and not nearly enough on concrete and consistent caring. Many men have been programmed to see themselves as necessarily the main economic provider and "head" of the home, religion, and society. These and other oppressive scripts frustrate growth within and between men themselves as well as with women.

More specifically, most men never learn to understand and to deal with a woman's anger. Many well-intentioned men avoid or withdraw from female anger; others attack the anger. In either approach—flight or fight—men have difficulty staying with the woman and listening to her. They fear rejection, are unable to accept conflict, or are afraid of being dominated. Whatever the reason, their inability to deal with angry women aborts communication and engenders more problems. It certainly would help men (and women) if they learned to appreciate angry women—and if women would help men to learn this skill.

A man may question himself: Can I be truly affectionate with others? Must I function in so-called masculine ways that exclude spontaneity, gentleness, and care? Can I share feelings and responsibilities with a woman? Can I be a househusband? Can I surrender to a woman? Can I listen to her anger? How can women help me? Where is the woman in me?

The childhood of men varies considerably and has a significant impact on their lives. "What were (and are) my parents like? Was my dad a 'phantom father'? Did he show affection and enjoy time with me, or did he spend time with me out of dutifulness? Was my mother overburdened with family responsibilities? How did she treat me? Did I always have to do 'masculine' things? Did I learn to see girls as inferior, fickle, and servile, or as domineering and cold? Was I taught that boys hide their fears and pain? How do I see girls or women now? Do I feel free to express my whole self? What is my view of being a true man?"

Men often think that the image of a man is much clearer and more set than a woman's. But is it? Is being an authentic man the same as being masculine? Masculinity is highly influenced by cultural programming; what is regarded as masculine in one culture is not regarded so in another. Does a true man never cry, never feel intense, rarely show his love? Is it "unmanly" to cook, to sew, or to do housework? What is an "androgynous man"?

Men may also be less certain of their identity because the influence of their mothers is stronger than that of their fathers. Some fathers seem to be working, golfing, bowling, reading, or just too busy or tired to be available. If this is true, a boy's preparation for being a man has been quite limited. Parenthetically, the absence of a mature man or father can also be detrimental to the growth of a woman.

Women can actually be more certain than men of their sexual identity. This may occur because mothers usually spend more time qualitatively and quantitatively with their children; consequently, women can be influenced more by their own sex. Of course, the mother's attitudes are significant in influencing the kind of woman the girl will become.

Along with the physical and functional dimensions, our primary sexuality also has a *spiritual* dimension. There is a strong tendency to consider sexuality and spirituality as mutually exclusive. Indeed, sexuality has often been despiritualized and spirituality has often been desexualized. However, both sexuality and spirituality are essential and interrelated dimensions of being human. A sexual person—male or female—is spiritual. Spirituality without sexuality dehumanizes the person.

Our spiritual life is influenced by the fact of our being a man or a woman. Personal history and cultural programming can have a decisive impact on spiritual growth. For example, if a man learns that spiritual experience is unimportant or secondary to functional achievement and success, he will have no incentive to spiritual growth. If a woman is programmed to take the backseat in spiritual leadership, she can sell herself short or be prevented from making her contribution. Throughout history, men and women have been community leaders in the field of spirituality, but women have seldom held public positions of power and leadership. Is this the best way?

Other spiritual issues can be reconsidered in light of primary sexuality. For instance, do men and women pray differently? Do men and women experience liturgy differently? Important differences may exist. Such differences, however, would be complementary because of our androgyny. For instance, we can explicate common and recurring themes in male and female spiritual writers. Still, there may be some differences due to both cultural and natural forces. Perhaps men and women experience and articulate spirituality in different but complementary ways.

Men often direct and control, at least externally, the spiritual lives of women. Are there dangers when only men set structures and plan programs for women's spirituality? Certainly men can help women's spiritual formation, but women may direct women (and men) differently and have a distinct impact on them. Furthermore, men may be constricted when they have access to only "male spirituality." It seems better to have a choice.

Consider the more functional, political, and ministerial aspects of religion. It is a particular danger to judge ministry only or primarily according to male models. The ministry and leadership of women in religious and spiritual domains is sometimes unnecessarily curtailed. A woman could minister just as significantly as a man, although somewhat differently. Presently women are "allowed" to promote spirituality and to have positions of authority in "their own" domains, but they could be given more opportunities to the benefit of both sexes. Indeed, women are entering various areas of spiritual ministry in greater numbers; one can hope this will be encouraged to continue.

One reason for sexist oppression in spiritual and religious matters is that women can intimidate men intellectually, sexually, and spiritually. Until recently, men had more and better formal religious education than women. A nun was seldom educated better than a priest, but now many religious and laywomen have acquired higher education. Kept out of traditional centers of religious education such as seminaries, women went to universities. These "naive, second-class" women often got as good or a better education than men. Furthermore, since they were in a heterosocial environment as contrasted with a homosocial environment, they had more concrete and constructive opportunities to cope with celibate heterosexuality. Perhaps the intellectual and sexual power of women intimidates men. Perhaps women's education, criticism, creativity, and heterosexual adjustment threaten some men to the extent that they must keep women in second place.

Although women comprise a majority portion of the spiritual infrastructure, seldom do they have superstructure positions of authority and opportunity. What would happen if men shared their power and responsibility, listened to and learned from women, and worked and prayed equally together? What would happen if women had more explicit influence in forming religious structures, guidelines, and policies? Perhaps new opportunities for spiritual growth would emerge.

Love, the paramount dynamic of spirituality, can also be considered in light of primary sexuality. Do men and women love differently? We have seen that men are usually able to separate love from other experiences and that women usually have more difficulty in being intimate with more than one man. Women are inclined to value and promote care more than principle, experience more than theory. Women's integral presence and tendency to promote love can be a positive and powerful influence on individual and communal spirituality. Unfortunately, some women minimize their own powerful presence and instead seek the questionable power of men. They try to follow a male model while minimizing or forgetting the essence of spirituality: love.

Perhaps the male propensity to be task-oriented has predisposed men to maximize the value of religious administration, problem solving, and rational theology, thus minimizing spiritual sensibility and experience. It seems men can be more easily programmed to pursue rational and theoretical knowledge, forgetting transrational experience. To talk about religion differs from fostering the spiritual essence of religion: love.

Finally, let's consider beautiful, *aesthetic* sexual people. They may be old, physically unattractive, and functionally impaired. Yet they are beautiful because their spirit speaks and is in harmony with their embodied selves. Old persons can be sexually beautiful because they radiate their dignity and wisdom. Crippled and deformed persons—men and women of integrity—are beautiful. People who manifest the spirit of life and promote harmonious, ongoing wholeness are beautiful men and women. The arthritic hands of an aging, healthy, and holy woman or man are more beautiful than the twenty year old's sensuous hands. The old hands tell a life story—the human story. They speak of joy and suffering, of intimacy and aloneness, of pleasure and pain, of good and evil, of success and failure, of you and me. They embody the spirit of everyone.

People who experience life aesthetically are, at least implicitly, in contact with the spiritual. A difference between the aesthetic and the spiritual is that the accent of beauty is on the dynamic whole, while spirituality focuses on the spirit of that whole. In short, aesthetic experience can foster spirituality and vice versa. It is not accidental that places of sacred worship usually incorporate symbols of beauty—objects like paintings and activities such as singing which can foster spiritual experiences.

To summarize: people are primarily male or female androgynous beings. This primary sexuality is experienced and manifested in physical, functional, spiritual, and aesthetic ways, and in combinations of these dimensions. We are challenged to become whole sexual selves, to foster the optimum conditions that promote androgynous, sexual, functional, and spiritual growth.

CHAPTER 4

Affective Sexuality

We have seen that all human activity is sexual insofar as we are men and women. Primary sexuality influences the way we perceive, think, feel, act, and interact. In short, our sex affects how we work, play, suffer, and enjoy.

Out of this basic sexuality emerges another essential mode of sexuality: affective sexuality, the dimension of interpersonal intimacy. Before we discuss the various experiences and dynamics of affective sexuality, let's consider some basic definitions and distinctions.

Affective sexuality refers to feelings, modes, and emotions ("affects") that move toward or incorporate *intimacy*. It describes how we are affectively (more than cognitively) motivated to become closer to one another—to "touch" physically, functionally, spiritually, or aesthetically. We feel "affection" for another; we desire to be closer to another.

In affective sexuality, a key word is "intimacy"—the experience of self-disclosure and sharing. We want to show and share ourselves as well as to see and receive the other. However, intimacy may be primarily physical without any long-term care or commitment, or it may involve deeper and lasting dimensions of our spiritual self. We can be "turned on," "tuned in," or involved for moments, hours, months, years, or a lifetime. Whatever the case, we yearn, desire, want, and need to be close to another.

Affective sexuality takes many forms. Depending on our intentions, feelings, and opportunities, our "feeling for" someone may motivate us to disclose and share ourselves in the close, permanent union of marital love or friendship, or it may be less affective and intimate as in a gracious meeting or warm recognition. To be sure, affective sexuality also represents a drive toward intimacy, although it may include or exclude affection.

The important distinction is that affective intimacy can be an end in itself, or it can be in service to and part of genital behavior. For instance, a warm smile or a respectful caress can be an end in itself, or it may lead to or be part of a genital encounter. Affective sexuality can stand on its own as a way of relating to another person, or it can be a prelude to genital activity. The failure to make this distinction causes unnecessary problems. When affective and genital sexuality are considered identical, or when affection is seen as necessarily leading to genital sex, frustrating confusion and fruitless guilt are among the possible consequences.

The primary way to determine if our affection is an end in itself or a means to genital sex is to examine our motives. As we will see, motivations are both conscious and unconscious, in both self and the other. I can be in conflict with my own intentions, or my intentions may conflict with yours, or vice versa. For example, I may sincerely intend to be only affectionate with you but find myself being genitally aroused. Or, you may be intimate with me without any genital desires, but I may become genitally aroused, or I may misinterpret your affection as an invitation to genital sex. One of us may find ourselves in a (genital) situation neither intended or desired. The challenge is to be aware of one's own as well as the other's intentions.

When affective sexuality leads to genitality in oneself, the other, or both, we can affirm the genital arousal and freely choose what course of action to take. A negative approach is to repress genital experiences or to cover the feelings they arouse with a veil of rationalization. The more open we are to the possibility of genital sex in affective encounters, the more able we are to creatively control genitality and choose whether or not to promote purely affective sexuality.

The experience of affective sexuality

Affective sexuality is clearly seen in its aesthetic dimension. "Affective aesthetic" sexuality incorporates both affective and aesthetic components so that feelings of intimacy are permeated with beauty. Consider a ballet that manifests the erotic and aesthetic: the performers show affection and aesthetic intimacy, and their dance is an end in itself. The dancers have no intention of using their erotic aesthetic dance as a means to genital sexuality; if their dance were used as a prelude to genital intimacy, it would take on a different tone and flavor. The dancers' intentions are to express and celebrate erotic and aesthetic intimacy solely as an end in itself.

On an everyday level, consider a man and a woman who dance with each other on an affective aesthetic plane. Although their dancing may not be objectively aesthetic, they feel beautiful and they become affectively intimate with each other. Their dancing can be an end in itself, or it can be an overture to genital relations. A married couple may dance in an erotic-aesthetic way as partly a prelude to genitality, while two friends enjoy a dance without genital intentions.

Problems emerge when the partners have different motivations—for instance, if a woman understands the dance as an end in itself but her partner uses it as an avenue to genital sex. Using the dance as a means, the man will probably become genitally aroused. Many women sense such intentions and consciously choose to cooperate or impede them. If she is unaware of his intentions, a woman will be surprised as he becomes more explicit in his genital pursuits; he may become frustrated and angry if she refuses to go along with his intentions.

It is also possible that a woman will misinterpret a man's intentions, thinking that dancing will lead to greater intimacy through a date or spending a night together. If the man has no such intentions, the woman will feel confused, hurt, frustrated, or angry when he leaves her. The man may be innocent, but he could be more aware of the woman's mood and intentions, and she of his. To prevent frustration, exploitation, or other pain, both partners should know their own and the other's intentions.

Again, a couple who intend their dance (or any affective behavior) to be an end in itself may discover themselves unintentionally becoming genitally stimulated. Denying such evidence, they may move toward direct or indirect satisfaction and feel frustrated and perhaps guilty. On the other hand they might step back (physically, psychologically, or spiritually) and take stock of their situation. They can decide to promote genital activation, suppress, sublimate, or integrate their feelings, or stop dancing.

There are other forms of aesthetic affective sexuality also. A literary example is some sacred Scriptures such as the Song of

Songs. The poetic passages of this book center primarily around life in love. The Song can be considered spiritual poetry that celebrates affective sexuality. Reading this work could be a prelude to genital intimacy, but can also proclaim the joy of intimacy without genitality.

A man and woman who appreciate each other as whole persons can have erotic feelings that are interwoven with aesthetic respect. Although such a relationship can lead to genital intimacy, it also can be an enjoyable experience in itself. It is possible for a man and a woman to be chaste and celibate lovers if they communicate their motives to one another.

Another couple may engage in deep care and self-revelation. However, one person intends this as a move toward deeper intimacy. The man may interpret this affective encounter as a step toward genital encounter, the woman as the beginning of a more consistent and longer lasting relationship. If the expectations of either are disappointed, both may be hurt. This unfortunate situation arises because a man may express himself in such an open and personal way that the woman concludes that he wants to promote the relationship. His open care and true affection can be justifiably interpreted as a promise for a future relationship, but in fact his intentions may not include this promise. The woman, seeking to pursue the relationship, will become confused, frustrated, and angry when he does not follow through. Ideally, a man should realize that his behavior can be misinterpreted and that he should make his intentions clear. A woman should be more assertive and proclaim her feelings and intentions.

Similar problems exist in marriage. One partner may want to express physical affection without genital relations; the other might misinterpret physical affection as a prelude to genital encounter. Women particularly like to embrace and to be physically intimate as a way of expressing affection. Such intimacy is highly sexual though not explicitly genital; too often men misinterpret this affection as a desire for genital encounter. When a woman thwarts the man's advances toward genital expression, both become frustrated, hurt, and angry. The key point here is that all physical affection need not and should not lead to genitality. A couple who hold and caress each other can have an intimate, pleasurable, and loving experience that need not lead to genital behavior.

The Western male is often seen as the bearer of genital sexuality, and the Western woman tends to be evaluated primarily as the guardian of affective sexuality. Since the culture of the United States usually considers erotic-aesthetic behavior as feminine or sentimental, people assume it is natural for a woman to be affectively aesthetic. However, when a man expresses erotic-aesthetic behavior, such as in the performing and fine arts, he may be considered effeminate or unmanly. The premise is that a "man" is defined as aggressive and controlled, not aesthetic. To be erotic-aesthetic, a man usually needs the support of a subculture such as a group of dancers or artists. When he behaves erotically and aesthetically, he may be ridiculed. This is sexist and actually does violence to men because they are and can be erotic-aesthetic.

Men are programmed to minimize affective sexuality as an end in itself, using it only or primarily as an approach to genital sexuality. When a man expresses affection, he feels pressured sooner or later to pursue genital relations. Consequently, a celibate man may abstain from affective expression to avoid genital involvement; an older man may minimize affection in order to avoid the "pressure to perform" genitally. Such performance anxiety is partly due to the feeling that affective sexual behavior is necessarily a prelude to genital behavior. To avoid embarrassment or guilt about genital arousal and the consequent pressure to perform, the man constricts his affective involvement with others.

Because of these and other reasons, women have learned to suspect or be confused by men. For instance, when a man expresses himself erotic-aesthetically, a woman will often hesitate and wonder what the man's true intentions are. As long as she hesitates or doubts the man, she cannot fully enter the relationship. Moreover, her doubts are often well-founded because a man frequently takes advantage of the trust a woman gives him. A man too often tries to "con" a woman on an affective level to "make" her on a genital level. On the other hand, the man experiences the woman as withdrawing from him; if he has no intentions to move toward genital activity, he may become confused and withdraw from her. If the man is using the situation as a prelude to genitality, the woman's withdrawal may be wise. Of course, women do not have the edge on vulnerability. A woman, sensing a man to be intimidated by affection, may foster such anxiety to control or hurt him. Whatever the situation, affective sexuality should show care and understanding; it should foster mutual enjoyment and growth, not exploitation, pain, or selfishness.

Affective sexuality can be primarily spiritual also. As in other modes of sexuality, aesthetic and spiritual sexuality are similar and often closely related. The key distinction is which dimension—the aesthetic or the spiritual—is accented. In spiritual affective sexuality the accent is on spirituality with affective components. The language of some spiritual writers, for instance, has a dominantly affective tone, as the following passage illustrates:

> *My heart burns with love. I desire to be with you, and I yearn to give my all to you, O Lord, my love. I want to embrace you with every fiber of my being and have you embrace me. Though I am unworthy, I am yours forever.*

Contrast this passage with one that is strongly cognitive:

> *A knowledge of God, which includes reading Scripture, is important in fostering one's spiritual life. If one does not reflect on the articulation of God, on God's Word, one loses an important source of spiritual sustenance and motivation.*

Interpersonal care can be another mode of spiritual affection. In this type of encounter, affection may be expressed silently, clearly, and firmly. A warm and gentle smile can include some affective sexuality. However, although the person feels the warmth of affection, the transaction may be highly spiritual. The smile is mainly an expression of care and affirmation; the affection is felt to be in the background. Another example is physical touch. When a son holds his father's arm or embraces him, affective sexuality can be present while remaining in service of spiritual gratitude. In situations like this, a comforting touch, a supportive caress, and a compassionate word can express feelings of intimacy that are unlikely to lead to genital arousal.

Unlike aesthetic and spiritual affective sexuality, affective sexuality can be primarily physical. Physical affection that is highly erotic and has no explicit spiritual or aesthetic influence can easily evoke and lead to genital involvement. Physical affective sexuality is healthy and good when care is its ultimate motivation, as in the case of a married couple. A physical and pleasurable encounter between them can possibly be an end in itself; it also can lead to a pleasurable genital encounter. However, their ultimate orientation is care for each other. This shows how persons can focus on each other's embodiment without treating each other as sex objects or as people to manipulate.

Genuine friends also can express physical affective sexuality. However, it can lead to genitality. Physical expressions of affection can pressure friends to behave genitally, especially when their care (or spirit) is more in the background than in the foreground. Behavior such as erotic dancing, sensuous touching, and using sexually seductive language can engender genital arousal. If and when such stimulation occurs, friends can decide what they will do—promote, suppress, limit, stop, sublimate, or integrate genital sex. Friends ought to be careful, to be ready to show their spirit, if they engage in erotic sexuality.

Physical affective sexuality is mad or bad when no care is present or intended. In this case, physicality is separated from functionality and spirituality. We treat the other as a sex object, as a merely physical being to satisfy our physical needs. To reiterate, this dissociative process is not healthy or good; we are more than physical beings. We embrace this dis-integrating approach when we engage in speech and flirting that exclude respectful care, participate in activities such as dancing that focus entirely on physical arousal, or choose modes of dress that maximize eroticism and immodesty. These and other forms of physical affective sexuality can promote genitality without care. Even if such activities do not culminate in genitality, frustration and anger result because the implicit promise of genital sex is not kept.

As in previous scenarios, individuals can have different intentions here, too. For instance, a man can contemplate a woman only in her physical dimension and act in a physically affective way to pressure her into genitality. The woman may sense this and stop the transaction, or she may encourage it. Similarly, a person's mode of behavior and dress may be intended to be aesthetically sexual, but be interpreted instead as an invitation to genital sexuality. It is important to know one's own and the other's intentions.

When the accent is on functionality, affective sexuality is illustrated in social behavior that involves qualities such as consideration and warmth. When a man acts as a gentleman and a woman as a lady, they show graceful consideration for others. Demonstrating a sense of humor or kidding another in a light and easy way involves affective sexuality. Some clothing styles may be aesthetically or physically affective, but some modes of dress are functionally affective also. Clothing, being a self-extension that indicates a way of living, draws attention through style, color, and presentation.

An example of functional affective sexuality is a woman acting as hostess at a social gathering. Her intention may not be and certainly does not have to be to deepen intimacy. Her behavior is neither explicitly spiritual nor primarily physical. Although it can be more or less aesthetic, the way she acts is mainly to serve a social and functional situation. She can be graceful and charming, warm and kind, considerate and friendly. Instead of being merely functional, task-oriented, and highly cognitive, she also behaves affectively. She shows she is a person of flesh and blood, not simply a cold function. Unfortunately, however, her affectivity can be misinterpreted as an overture to more intimate relations, since men are prone to assume that affectivity, especially in a social situation, is a come-on.

Similarly, a man acting as a waiter shows functional affective sexuality. His sexuality is not directed toward more intimacy nor is it explicitly spiritual or aesthetic. Although his service may be an art, it is also a function. He shows a sophisticated style, is socially gracious, and perhaps entertains his patrons. Without affective sexuality, he would behave as a robot—as a cold function rather than as a warmly functional person.

Outside a marital context, affective sexuality should be an end in itself; it should not be a means to promote genital sexuality. Within marriage, affective sex that serves or is part of genital sexuality can promote healthy growth. Moreover, marital affective sex can and should be appropriate as an end in itself also. Lay single, vowed celibate, and married people (except with their spouse) can practice all forms of sexuality except genital behavior.

Heterosexual intimacy

Opposite-sex relationships and interaction evoke experiences that differ from same-sex or homosocial relationships and interaction. A man not only acts differently in the company of a woman; he also can learn from her in ways that he cannot or seldom learns from a man. Likewise, a woman manifests herself differently when she is with men and is affected differently by men than by her homosocial relationships. Men without women and women without men fail to become whole persons. Let us consider, then, the problems, challenges, and opportunities of heterosexual intimacy.

A man and woman dining together can be a healthy and enjoyable encounter. If their dining is regular and private, the relationship may move from friendship to dating and encourage more intimacy. Private, romantic settings regularly enjoyed usually promote experiences that engender desire for greater intimacy, including genital intimacy. If the man and woman are vowed celibates or married to another, they can be honest with themselves and responsible toward each other by knowing their possibilities and limits in the situation. Otherwise, "love games" under the cloak of friendship may emerge, or greater intimacy is promised but not delivered.

Nevertheless, this man and woman can and should express their primary and affective sexuality. If they repress their affective sexuality, they can become cold and insipid. They may speak good lines, but they will lack the "touchability" and spirit of caring persons. Consequently their dining will become boring and contrived. If the couple minimize or repress their spiritual selves, they try to be only physical and/or functional—and ultimately less alive than they can be.

When we promote the physical erotic and exclude the spiritual component of affective sexuality, we may evoke genital desires that lead to either frustration or carry through. For example, a party can and should include healthy affective sexuality. A gathering, however, that promotes the physical-erotic and represses the aesthetic and spiritual fosters an increase of physical and/or genital intimacy. In short, intimate physical dancing, erotic flirting, genital talk, touching games, and promotion of erotic fantasy can generate the erotic-genital rather than the erotic-aesthetic—

or a more integrated sexual presence.

Whether we are unmarried (single, religious, or priest) or married (who are celibate except in relation to one person), we need to love others and be committed to healthy and holy living. Imagine a religious brother and sister who are friends. Their friendship occasionally moves them toward erotic and genital intimacy. They express their love erotically in a loving glance or in a chaste touch, but they are careful that their eroticism is interwoven with aesthetic and spiritual qualities. Facing each other as whole persons, their erotic feelings are less likely to promote genitality. When their intimacy does evoke genitality, they set limits because of the absence of marital commitment and because of their love and religious commitments. They neither repress nor satisfy their erotic and genital desires; they affirm their desires and freely choose not to promote and realize them. At times they may be frustrated and dislike their "no," but they freely, though perhaps reluctantly, put limits on the kind of sexual contact they will share. Their "no" is based on a more fundamental "yes"—a yes to their values, love, and primary commitment. This same resolve can characterize the sexual choices of single and married persons.

It is possible to hold false notions of chastity and celibacy that impede growth in intimacy. Chastity does not mean sexlessness; it is an experience of integrated (whole) and chaste (pure) loving sex. Chaste persons see and relate to others and self as whole beings, not as fragmented persons. By isolating physical, functional, or even spiritual modes of perception and behavior from one another, individuals become less than they are. They become "impure"—not being their true and/or "pure" selves.

Heterosexual intimacy can be especially problematic for people who have repressed their sexuality or who are sexually immature. Consider the example of a man who represses his sexuality and enters a heterosexual relationship. Though he cares deeply, he may be ripped with conflict: his repressed sexual needs strongly seek satisfaction, while his standards deny awareness of these desires. Continued repression causes stress and its debilitating symptoms, while building up a slush fund of frustrated sexuality makes him vulnerable to more stress and to sudden gratification. If gratification occurs, he could feel liberated and discover a sense of well-being that perhaps he never had. Feeling so accepted and at ease, he may find himself drifting to the opposite extreme: intensively craving genital gratification.

Another example is a woman sexually fixated in adolescence. Although she has not actively repressed her sexuality, she is sexually immature because she has never had much opportunity to explore, understand, and integrate sex. If she becomes involved with a man, she will probably experience sexual desires that her adolescent attitudes fail to integrate. She may act as an adolescent and/or become too dependent on the man, minimizing her autonomy. Or being naive, she may become a prime candidate for exploitation. Unnecessary confusion and guilt could be evoked. Whatever happens, her challenge is to work through her psychosexual fixation before she becomes more involved or terminates the relationship.

When we attempt to work through sexual repression or fixation and sexual desires surface too quickly and intensely to integrate, a common consequence is to feel guilty. This is because our standards are incongruent with our experiences. We experience the painful conflict of intensely feeling one way and just as intensely thinking the opposite. Again, the challenge is to listen to both our thoughts and our feelings and come to a healthier resolution.

Conversely, some of us behave as though we are guiltless. We reason that "if it feels right, it is right." Although it is true that feelings seldom lie, their truth is not always the best truth. The popular ethic, "if it feels right, go for it," can be quite dangerous and destructive to self and others. Violence, addiction, manipulation, and well-intentioned but wrong behavior are justified by this philosophy. Using the comfort principle, we can change our ethical standards and justify extramarital genital sex.

Some say that if we are sincere and honest, then our behavior is good. Although honesty and sincerity are ways to truth, the "honesty and sincerity" syndrome can serve self-gratification as well as the truth of love. For instance, an individual can sincerely and honestly exploit another, or can be consciously sincere and honest but unconsciously use another. We can hide selfish intentions behind a facade of honesty and rationalize questionable behavior with a plea of sincerity. We can sincerely and honestly violate our love for each other. Simply stated, mad and/or bad behavior can be sincere and honest.

It is important to appreciate one another's values, standards, and development. Although certain behavior may be healthy for oneself, it may be inappropriate or negative for another. For instance, a married couple may have different attitudes toward certain sexual activities such as cunnilingus, fellatio, and anal stimulation. Also, two people may both be sexually immature, but in different ways. An example is the man who has difficulty with foreplay or the woman who docilely submits to fast sex without much emotional involvement. Both persons need to improve themselves and to help each other.

Another challenge of heterosexual intimacy is celibate heterosexual love. This can be more difficult for married people than for celibates. Unlike celibates, married persons commit themselves to each other. When a spouse regularly spends private time in a relationship outside the marriage, the latter relationship can gradually edge toward greater intimacy. Furthermore, such married persons take time and energy away from their main commitment; this can retard growth in their marriage.

An illustration of this possibility is a man who informs his wife that he is going to dine with a new female employee. He tells her that the woman is lonely and needs help to adjust to her new job and living situation. He feels sincerely obliged to help her. His wife, though perhaps hesitant and ambivalent, initially accepts this situation. But if the man calls his wife a few nights later explaining that the new employee is still lonely and requires his support, his wife probably will begin to feel more uncomfortable. She knows intuitively that such situations nurture deeper intimacy and, by taking time and space, hinder the spousal intimacy she has a right to expect. This does not mean that married people cannot have friends besides their spouse. Indeed, married persons can and should have friendships based on primary and affective sexuality as long as these do not impede or violate marital growth. To understand this better, it is good to take a close look at friendship in relation to sexuality.

Friendship

Virtually everyone wants to have and to be a friend. Some people are seeking to escape loneliness and boredom; some measure their personal success by the number of their friends—they feel guilty or ashamed if they have no friends; others, more cautious, withdraw from potential friendships because of fear or uncertainty. Some people believe that friendship is necessary to live a significantly meaningful life; others are open to friendship but feel content without intimate ones. Finally, there are people who maintain and nourish their friendships throughout their lives.

Friendship comes in various degrees and kinds. Some friends grow closer throughout their lifetime, others are friends at certain times in their lives. Some friends like to be with each other in any situation. Others enjoy each other primarily at work or at social gatherings (functional affective sexuality). Some friends genuinely play together but do not suffer together. All of these can be true friendships and can involve various modes of sexuality. A friendship where two persons share everything with trust, dependability, respect, and fidelity is relatively rare. Such a friendship can evoke the most painful problems including sexual ones, and yet it can have the greatest rewards. Having more than three or four of these friendships is improbable. One is enough.

The love that characterizes friendship wants to give to and help the other beyond the call of duty. Mutual care involves standing by, counting on, supporting, and defending each other not only in the easy and enjoyable times but also in the difficult and risky times. We muster the courage to be available to each other no matter what. Like other forms of love, authentic friendship is an end in itself; it needs no justification. As friends, we do not look for special gains or rewards; neither do we seek approval or a safe way of being liked or affirmed. True friendship is not parasitic. Rather, it strives toward unconditional and respectful concern for the other. Our friendship is a chaste love.

Unchaste friendship involves manipulation and/or exploitation. For example, a dependent man may satisfy a "friend's" need to dominate as well as his own need to be dependent. Such a relationship is unchaste because it is based on mutual need satisfaction rather than on giving to and supporting each other's welfare. Instead of promoting healthy growth, these individuals become fixated in a submissive-domineering relationship. Although such a relationship may not seem unchaste compared to sexist and/or genital exploitation, it is nevertheless *non castus*— not pure. Indeed, if perfection is the ideal, probably all relation-

ships are more or less unchaste. Our challenge is to "purify" ourselves—to uncover and control our hidden unchaste motives.

In our best friendships, whether heterosocial or homosocial,
we ought to express our primary sexuality and to interact affectively with each other as well. An assertive statement, a nourish-
ing support, a warm glance, an assuring touch, or a respectful
embrace can demonstrate concern for the other. Genital relations
also can be a meaningful and enjoyable expression of love, but
intuition (as well as clinical and empirical evidence) tells us that
genital relations change our friendship and potentially destroy it.
Genital intercourse is one mode of intimate relationship, but celibate friendship can be just as intimate without genital behavior.
Although we may sometimes yearn for genital relations, we can
freely choose—albeit with painful reluctance—to say no to genital encounter in service of a yes to our love.

In a certain sense, every deep and authentic friendship is particular. As friends we see each other unlike anyone else sees us;
we have and are something special. Such intimate friendships are
especially available to and fruitful for celibates. Being free from
the marital commitment to another human being (particularly in
regard to time and space) can allow celibates to be free for intimate friendships. Although married people may have intimate
friendships outside marriage, there is the danger that such friendships, especially heterosexual ones, can hinder the growth of
their marital relationship. Perhaps married persons should foster
their particular and exclusive friendship within the marriage. In a
sense, a married person's best friend should be his or her spouse.

Romantic love and sexuality

Romantic love is in many ways the most exciting mode of
love. It is the love of romance writers, of youth, of the infatuated.
It is a love that activates all our senses; it is never dull or mun-
dane.

Romantic love is exciting and secretive. Feeling intensely and
often erotically attracted, the one smitten is strongly involved
with the ideal. Romantic lovers idealize each other at first, feeling they can do and share anything and be their most perfect
selves. They feel what love can be without its limits—and they
want to give, to be, and to receive all that is possible. There is a

special magic; romantic love can be so intense and total that it can sometimes seem a fantasy that will disappear at any moment.

What happens when we fall romantically in love? Initially we feel as though we are walking on clouds and that everything is possible. We experience the other as "perfect"; imperfections are secondary at best. We may feel we want to live together forever and consequently get married to capture this love forever. The romantic stage of marital love is one of the most exciting, pleasurable, and satisfying experiences.

Friendships also can have a romantic period. We experience new possibilities in testing our limits, risk our vulnerability, feel more alive than ever before, and are willing to do almost anything. We may feel that everything is possible and all right, and that life is rich and full. Romantic friendship usually inspires us to become our best selves; new energy and courage provide the way.

Romantic experiences are possible even in solitude. For instance, we may feel intensely the spiritual possibilities of contemplation. Or we may discover a world of meaning that is transcendent and permanent. Asking ultimate questions and being confronted with mysterious issues can engender a peak experience.

Romantic lovers—vowed celibate, single, or married—initially experience the unlimited potential of each other and celebrate each other's perfection. However, paradise does not last; romantic time is usually followed by the jarring revelation of imperfections, and perhaps withdrawing from each other.

It is not uncommon for an engaged couple, radiating love, to begin doubting their love after the honeymoon period. Having once divinized each other, they now demonize each other. Minor habits become irritating: one squeezes the toothpaste from the middle, the other from the end. His snoring upsets her; her hair curlers annoy him. More serious, she becomes frustrated and angry because he no longer shows his feelings as he once did. He becomes confused and angry with her constant complaining about his overinvolvement in work and his unavailability. Whatever the focus of criticism, they concentrate on each other's limitations instead of on the bright possibilities.

Another example is a person who experiences the religious life as a perfect way of living. Particularly in early formation when there is considerable personal affirmation, exploration, and direction, religious life offers extraordinary opportunities for individual and communal growth. However, problems may rise when the new religious moves from the novitiate into an ordinary community. Community living is much different here than in the novitiate or its idealization in vocation literature. Discovering the inevitable imperfections of others will feel more like a burden than a joy. Here again, the danger is to identify religious life or any way of life with its limits and obstacles. There are both problems and opportunities in any personal or professional life.

Imagine two persons who care for each other and become close friends. At first, they may idealize their relationship so that it becomes exclusive. They will wonder how they ever lived without each other. If one or both of them have been inhibited in expressing affection, they feel free now to express themselves without restraint. They feel liberated and more wholly alive. However, this "particular" friendship soon encounters limits and obstacles. For instance, the friends discover they can irritate and confuse each other; they can become hurt, angry, and perhaps guilty and ashamed. Instead of withdrawing from the situation, both persons should step back and listen to themselves and each other, then hopefully return to renew and deepen their friendship so it includes both their positive and negative dimensions.

The challenge and ideal is that both light and dark sides of life be integrated; neither should be absolutized. In fact, these experiences point to and affirm what life is: both divine and demonic, light and dark, creative and destructive. When we experience a person as perfect, we should remind ourselves that every person is imperfect. When we have disagreements, we should recall past agreements and perhaps agree to disagree. We are challenged to see potential virtue where there is vice, strength where there is weakness, joy where there is sadness, love where there is hate, life where there is death. Courage and vision are needed to move with and grow from life's paradoxical rhythm.

Affective sex is a part of romantic love that is—and should be—particularly enjoyable. But the desire to give one's self totally to another person can present difficulties. The affective and ideal qualities of romantic love drive us toward abandoning all and any limits; consequently, we yearn to give ourselves unconditionally in every way possible. As celibates we can long to celebrate our love in genital experiences, but we can say "no" in service of a "yes" to our love.

Ideally, a radical decision or a life commitment should not be made in either the so-called divine or demonic phases of love. When we are madly in love and experience no imperfections whatsoever—the divine phase—a life commitment is precarious. We should be just as prudent about making radical decisions while in a demonic phase: when life is overwhelmingly dark, any light or relief is tempting. However, it is better to wait until light emerges within the present situation—to wait until we can make more sense of our struggle and be freer to choose. For example, a person who is jilted or betrayed quickly becomes emotionally involved on the "rebound," being especially vulnerable to understanding and affection. This individual can impulsively make decisions he or she will regret later.

Ideally, we also should not make a life decision within the context of romanticism or fantasy. Romanticism knows no limits or imperfections, and a life decision requires that we be open to the limitations set by both the positive and negative factors of our past, present, and future situations. For instance, a man who falls in love with a woman may be in the divinizing stage of romantic love. When asked what is wrong with his beloved, he may offer nothing concrete. Until he can point out experientially what is positive and negative about her and himself, it is better that he wait before making such a radical decision to get married or remain single.

Conversely, it is tempting to separate when nothing seems right or possible. Experiencing enormous stress, we can be duped into feeling that a change in life-style will solve personal problems. More likely, we will take our problems with us. It is wiser to look at and deal with the dark side in and between ourselves before making decisions.

Authentic committed love is never perfect or divine, but neither is it merely imperfect or demonic. It is a combination of both. If authentic love were perfect, commitment would not be necessary. Because we are a composite of perfections and imperfections, commitment is called for.

Romantic love is important, however, because it can be a prelude to a more committed love. Its power of attraction, gentle excitement, and erotic idealism makes it easier, more enjoyable, and exciting for us to enter love. Since love, especially intimate love, is a risky venture, romantic love makes the entry into love relatively easier, safer, and more fun. Romantic love is an intense promise of a more permanent love that is both ideal and limited, erotic and transcendent, for the moment and forever, pleasurable and painful, divine and demonic—in short, a love that embraces and dignifies all of us.

This does not mean that romantic love is only a means toward an end. When immersed in romantic love, it is good to celebrate and proclaim it in the world. Our experience is a witness to love and often promotes happiness for others. Moreover, it offers a precious source of memories that can help us regain perspective when going through difficult times. Indeed, as authentic lovers we can consistently, if not constantly, celebrate our love romantically.

An affectionate disposition

An affectionate disposition refers to a readiness to love everyone and anyone, anywhere, at any time, and as much as possible. Although we cannot be open to everyone at the same time, we can express love to people we see every day, once a year, or less. Such a loving orientation is normally expressed in the day-to-day activities of work, play, impromptu meetings, and social gatherings. Thoughtfulness, respect, courtesy, compromise, genuine concern, warmth, understanding, and compassion can be manifestations of an everyday disposition of affection.

The disposition to love is a key dynamic in good and healthy loving. When the opportunity arises, those having this disposition are ready to express affection in the best possible way. They are willing to promote another's welfare as best they can by being friendly, doing a favor, or even withdrawing. (Paradoxically, to withdraw from another can sometimes be the best way to love that person. If saying something does more harm than good, perhaps staying out of a person's way for awhile is the best form of intimacy. Sometimes giving nothing more than a friendly smile or detaching oneself from another's problems instead of futilely trying to solve them can be the best form of love.)

Everyday affection is seldom intense and directly intimate;

when it is, we should take responsibility for it. It is unfair to share deeply, then suddenly leave or withdraw. Such intimacy can imply that more love is to come. This unfulfilled promise can breed pain and resentment. For example, Jane may be sincerely concerned about Joan who is lonely. In the name of love, she listens to Joan's frustrations and helps her realize herself in intimacy. But when Joan grows in love and begins to seek a friendship based on a two-way rather than a one-way relationship, Jane may suddenly set limits or withdraw. Jane, for positive and/or negative reasons, may be unwilling or unable to receive what Joan wants to give. For sure, everyday affection can lead to an intimate form of love such as friendship. When it does, we should be willing to take the time and effort to respond justly and honestly rather than making implicit promises we do not intend to or cannot fulfill.

It is usually better to know one another well before beginning to foster the physical or the spiritual dimensions of affective sexuality. Failing this can be intrusive or chauvinistic. For instance, after knowing a man for an hour, a woman may try to encounter him spiritually. If the man does not intend this kind of direct care as he might in a counseling situation or with a friend, he could feel spiritually raped. On the other hand, we can sometimes find ourselves immediately at home with each other and feel safe enough to move closer without conventional preliminaries. This is not the normal process, but it can happen.

Chaste affective sexuality

Unfortunately, chastity is culturally interpreted as an impediment to or repression of sexuality. In fact, chastity promotes and nourishes healthy behavior for it combats our tendencies to be selfish, exploitative, and manipulative.

Consider chastity in its basic sense as respectful and unconditional concern. As chaste persons, we act with respect: we take a second look at reality and seek its deeper meaning. We take this initiative when we look at life with care. Rather than experiencing one another only as physical or functional beings, we strive to see, appreciate, and respond to our whole personhood. And remember, to see people as disembodied—only as spiritual—can also be unchaste. To repress one's sexuality, for example, can be an unchaste act. To separate sexuality from spirituality, or spirituality from sexuality, is unchaste. Chastity means to experience and to respect another as a whole person. Chastity is the virtue by which sexuality and spirituality are dynamically interrelated.

A chaste person tries to promote what is good because it is good and strives to give for the sake of giving. Not acting to get what can be got from others, he or she does what should be done because it is right. Chastity involves behaving with unconditional care, without the impurities of exploitation and manipulation. Chaste persons try to purge themselves of hidden agendas. Chaste behavior is pure.

Chastity demands that we transcend such impurities as lust, manipulation, exploitation, arrogance, selfishness, and pride. Acting out of physical desires alone is unchaste because it involves treating ourselves and others only as physical beings. Manipulation for self-satisfaction is also unchaste because it lacks concern and respect. Likewise, exploitation and patronizing on any sexual level—primary, genital, or affective—is unchaste. For example, a man may be unchaste when he oppresses, pulls rank, or withdraws from a woman; a woman may be unchaste when she is masochistic, obsequious, or hostile. Rather than manipulating or using one another, we should take care to respond integrally: physically, functionally, spiritually, and aesthetically.

Chastity also can help us to purge negative defense mechanisms. For instance, we are not chaste simply because we abstain from genital gratification. To undervalue ourselves as men or women, to rigidly control affective sexuality, or to repress genital sexuality are modes of unchaste behavior. Indeed, to behave as sexless people violates chastity.

Willfulness or passive dependence can also be violations of chastity. When we inordinately depend on others for affection or sexual satisfaction, or try to please and serve them to manipulate their satisfaction of our needs, we are unchaste. Sucking the life out of people, we do anything as long as we are accepted and cared for. Living this way, we invite and encourage exploitation, although perhaps unconsciously. Passive and dependent persons can be unchaste in genital, affective, and primary sexuality. For instance, a woman who invites a man to dominate or manipulate her is unchaste. A woman who encourages a man to exploit her genitally (even within marriage) is unchaste along with the man.

To submit to any form of sexual exploitation can be a normal and mad mode of false chastity—it is behavior that violates and insults human integrity.

Chastity requires discipline and freedom. Discipline involves creative control of one's life—to practice ways that promote the free expression of truth. Chaste persons are dedicated to awareness and control of the impurities that prevent them from being their best selves. They are careful to avoid either overestimating or underestimating the value of self and others. Interpersonally, they break through normal facades and games to become more available to others. Their freedom from the pollution of bias, egoism, and neediness frees them for love.

Unchaste sexual behavior means that the centripetal (centralizing) force of mere sex, especially genital sex, impedes or destroys the centrifugal (outgoing) movement of unconditional care. Loveless sex is unchaste because it works against healthy and integrated interpersonal relations. However, sex without care is not the only form of unchastity. The will-to-power expressed in exploitation can be just as lethal as loveless and perfunctory genital sexuality.

We have seen that chastity is necessary for healthy and holy living. However, some lay people consider vowed chastity and celibacy senseless. One reason religious vow chastity is to underline the importance and significance of chastity for everyone.

Nevertheless, vowed celibates can be unchaste in subtle ways as well as explicit ones. For example, the priest who counsels the lonely, frustrated, and attractive woman may be unchaste; his apparent concern for a woman's welfare may in fact conceal an attempt to satisfy his own needs. To probe her inner life, especially her sexual life, can satisfy his own needs while giving him a sense of being "holy." It is not holy, however; such countertransference is unchaste because it primarily serves the self and not others.

Perhaps as many offenses against chastity are committed within marriage as outside of it. For instance, sexual intercourse without love is unchaste. To defend herself and protest against such sexual barbarism, a woman may become sexually dysfunctional—perhaps the only way she can say no to a man's unchaste behavior. A man is also unchaste when he pulls rank on his wife or takes her for granted. Men have been programmed culturally to place women in roles of service to men. Their sexist expectations are unchaste.

A married woman's unchaste sexual behavior may be more subtle. Perhaps she treats her husband like a son or another child. She may be frequently flirtatious or suggestive, yet consistently withdraw from deep intimacy. She may withhold her affective sexuality from service of genital relations. She may use genital sexuality to manipulate her husband: instead of confronting him with the real issues, she punishes him by refusing genital sex. Moreover, she may say, "If you do what I say, then I will satisfy you." If he accedes, both partners of the contract are unchaste.

In many ways, lay celibates may have the more difficult time practicing chastity. Unlike married or religious persons, single persons usually do not have the support and affirmation of a community. In the throes of loneliness, single persons may feel pressure to seek immediate sexual fulfillment without committed love. In the next chapter we will see that although sex without love can be a pleasurable and satisfying experience, the fulfillment is temporary and it fails to promote wholistic growth.

Single women are particularly susceptible to unchaste treatment. Too many men are willing to take advantage of a woman's loneliness and, offering a caricature of care, stimulate her romantically. Of course, women can encourage such exploitation or even actively exploit. Recreational sex seems better than nothing. Although unchaste behavior may be normal, human, and meaningful, it is not healthy or good.

Chastity is a virtue that promotes a good and healthy life. Consequently, both married and nonmarried people ought to encourage chastity; religious celibates should live their vow and bear witness to its meaning.

Chaste people, married or unmarried, are respectful and loving people. They abstain from exploitative, manipulative, and deceptive behavior. They do not regard sexuality as something to use or as simply a source of pleasure. Rather, they see and celebrate in chastity the mystery—the spirit—of sex.

CHAPTER 5

Genital Sexuality

A common and mistaken tendency is to identify sexuality with genitality. Books and articles about sex are usually about genital sex. Such impoverished understandings of sex are unfortunate because, as we have noted, there are other kinds of sex as well. Genital sex is one of three types, but it has been overemphasized at the expense of the others. Consequently, many people are led to believe that they must gratify, alone or with another, their genital needs to avoid becoming frustrated, abnormal, or stupid.

Sexual standards have changed considerably in the past twenty years. Not long ago, many people followed a code of sexual repression; today, freedom without constraint is encouraged. Both of these extremes—the new sexual license and the old sexual bondage—are unhealthy. We turn now to consider healthy as well as immature ways of dealing with genital desires: the consequences of positive and negative approaches, the appeal and effects of experiences such as masturbation, pornography, and intercourse, and how genital feelings can promote wholistic growth without requiring genital behavior. Before discussing these specific topics, however, let us consider some normative structures and dynamics of genital sexuality.

Normative structures and dynamics

Genital sexuality is best defined as behavior, thoughts, fantasies, desires, and feelings that activate the genital organs. A distinction should be made between genital feelings (or genitality) and genital behavior. Genital intercourse and masturbation, for example, are explicit forms of genital behavior; desires and fantasies that may or may not lead to genital gratification are modes of genitality. Genital feelings and thoughts can be realized in behavior, but this is not necessarily so. Everyone, more or less, has genital feelings; these feelings need not be acted upon in genital behavior. In short, feelings are neutral, but what we do with our feelings determines healthiness or nonhealthiness.

Genital sexuality should be an articulation of the whole person; by itself, it is an essential part of ourselves that is related to but not the same as our whole selves. When we identify the human person with genital sex alone, we risk treating ourselves and others as less than we really are. Genital sex is one important expression—not the totality—of primary sex; that is, of being a man or a woman. If somebody looks at you only as a body which can give him or her satisfaction, that person is insulting you. After all, you are and have more than a body.

When we misuse or abuse genital sexuality, we violate ourselves. To use someone's body merely for gratification is to mistreat that person; it is to act as if the other is only "a body"—a "some-body." But when we actualize our genitality in healthy ways, we celebrate and actualize ourselves. Healthy genital sex involves care for the whole person—body, mind, and spirit—and not just "a body."

Central to this analysis is the understanding that genital sexuality contains a dynamic force that urges the individual to go beyond self to others. This transcendent movement in genital sex (as in all forms of sex) points to its relational quality. Genitality seeks more than self; it extends toward another. Genital sexuality urges us to seek union with others, and its healthy form lies in love.

Recall how genital organs change when a person is sexually aroused. They (ourselves) move toward the other to give and receive. The penis and clitoris as well as other sex organs seek contact, connection, and union with someone beyond themselves. The stimulation need not be merely physical; just as often or more so it is cognitive, affective, and spiritual. Genital changes are visible confirmation of the desire to be "in union with."

Sexuality is a sign that we are more than individuals, that we tend toward community. This unitive, transcendent movement can be considered the spiritual dimension of sexuality. Moreover, genital sexuality is one of the clearer signs of spirituality—of our call to love. In genital intercourse, two people go out to and receive each other. The spirit of genital sex powerfully urges us to be one with another, to give oneself and consequently to be more fully oneself.

Along with seeking union or love, (genital) sex fosters life. We seek communion, but procreation can be included as well. This is not to assert that the primary or only reason for genital intercourse is to have a child, but to point out that the possibility of procreation also bears witness to the transcendence or sacredness of genital sex. The possibility of conception affirms that in genital sex we go beyond our individual selves, and the inability to procreate implies the normative ability. Any attempt to control the possibility of procreation affirms its existence.

Genitality manifests clearly the transcendent dynamic and/or spiritual quality of sexuality. To nurture this thirst to go beyond ourselves, to grow individually and to foster community, a genuine commitment of love is necessary. Only love (spirit) is sufficient to meet the (spiritual) demands of genital sex. Only steadfast love can keep the transcendence of genitality in harmony with healthy growth. Physical satisfaction or psycho-social adjustments are inappropriate, inadequate responses to the demanding call of genital sex. Without the spiritual dimension, genital sex eventually dissipates into anxious emptiness. Indeed, genital behavior can be fun and meaningful without love, but it is not healthy. It starves the spirit as one futilely tries to nourish oneself with satisfaction and success. Being less than whole (and therefore less than healthy), the individual ends up being isolated rather than in communion.

Along with transcendence, sex involves embodiment. Consequently, it necessarily involves *time* and *space*. Too often, we minimize the importance of the obvious: since we are embodied and/or situated spirits, healthy genital sex requires a proper time and space. When people do not have or take the proper time for healthy genital sex, their experience is usually impeded and often causes distress.

For example, a married couple chooses to enjoy sex in the morning before their busy routines begin. Rushing their genital gratification, they will create an experience far from what it could and should be. Interestingly, the sexes usually have different needs in this regard. Women, for instance, can be especially sensitive to rushed and careless sex; men, though not all, engage more easily in "hurried sex."

A woman's primary sexuality inclines her to integrate her genital experience with other experiences such as love and affection; this process usually takes more time. A man, however, is prone to separate his experiences and/or to focus exclusively on genital sex. This process takes less time. Consequently, when a man pressures a woman to "hurry," she will usually feel tense or turned off. If genital sexuality is performed quickly, it soon loses its vitality and spirit. For sure, mere physical satisfaction can occur quickly, but an encounter between persons usually takes time. Embodiment means that time is important in giving oneself to another.

Here are one woman's comments on hurried sex: "Yes, sometimes we indulge in intercourse, but usually we just make out. Actually, I don't really care for mere genital sex. Sometimes it's exciting, but mainly it leaves me empty and frustrated. Sex simply doesn't fulfill me and, besides, it leaves me wanting. What really turns me off is when my boyfriend insists on having sex. It seems so urgent to him like nothing else matters—including me. It's like we have a deadline to meet. The whole thing turns me off."

As embodied persons, we need not only sufficient time but also the right space to foster and enjoy the sacred (love) dimension of genital sex. "Car sex" may be fun initially, but it soon becomes physically and psychologically cramped. An apartment or a pleasure resort may offer more comfort, but this situation is usually tentative and perhaps precarious. The lack of a place where a couple can feel secure and at home will eventually evoke tension that impedes healthy sexuality.

The lack of appropriate time and space for healthy genital behavior results eventually in distress. If nothing else, such genital sex becomes unwieldy. When couples find themselves planning genital relations, regulating the time, or hurrying the experience, they soon become tense and frustrated. Being discreet, moving from place to place, or planning meetings becomes tiring and contrived. Scheduling sex works against the rhythm and nurturance of healthy sex. Secure, comfortable time and space are needed for two persons (body, mind, and spirit) to encounter each other. Even when sex is a merely physical encounter, the individuals are left wanting more of each other. Healthy sex calls for love and affection; these take more time and better space than mere physical sex affords. Instead of being an integral and healthy part of life, such sex becomes too special and dissociated from the rest of life.

Only a marital situation can offer the proper time and appropriate place for healthy sexual relations. Premarital and extramarital sex can be meaningful and pleasurable, but the scheduling of time and finding a space build distress that impedes ongoing growth. Even if there is love, such genital expressions will, in the long run, hinder the growth of love. Yes, nonmarital sex can be an expression and affirmation of love, but the situation impedes the free progress of love; it can even destroy it. On the other hand, marriage does not always provide appropriate time and place either; nor does it guarantee healthy sex. Nevertheless, marriage—unlike nonmarital life-styles—is the only context wherein the proper time and place (on a long-term basis) are available to foster healthy and loving genital relations.

As noted earlier, genital sex is not only a pleasurable encounter or sacred mode of communication. In sex, we go beyond ourselves and out to another. In genital relations we are called to be responsible to each other not only for the moment but also for a lifetime. Genital sex invites a lifetime commitment of fidelity and love. The intimacy of genital sex is so immanent and transcendent that it can only be nurtured with the immanence and transcendence of love. Lacking the fidelity of love lived and nurtured in the proper time and appropriate space, the health of nonmarital genital relations, though meaningful, will in time dissipate rather than grow.

The normative principle is this: when we lack a permanent commitment of fidelity and love as well as the time and space that marriage offers, genital relations fail to promote healthy (wholistic) growth. Though nonmarital sex may be meaningful and satisfying, it does not engender ongoing, wholistic growth. The necessary components for healthy sex are proper time, appropriate place, and commitment; these can be found only in marriage.

However, living life is not as simple as theorizing about it. It can be difficult to abstain from genital sex, especially when in the throes of love. Knowing that sex outside of marriage will not foster healthy growth may seem a weak and abstract reason when faced with the immediate rewards of genital expression.

Having considered the normative principles, let us consider the clinical/pastoral sense and nonsense of genital behavior.

Motivations for genital gratification

Motivation describes the "why," "how," and "what for" of behavior. Motivations are forces—feelings, attitudes, and biological-dynamics—that urge us to act in one way rather than another. Let us consider some reasons, positive and negative, for having and not having sex. Most of these reasons can be healthy, nonhealthy, or both.

Satisfaction and pleasure

A common motivation for genital behavior is to satisfy needs, reduce tension, and experience pleasure. Orgasm, for instance, makes one feel at ease, without tensions or needs, at rest. Instead of promising a delayed or long-term reward, genital gratification gives immediate pleasure. Genital sex with self or another is especially tempting when we feel urgently the need to be fulfilled. And fulfillment is possible. But without committed love in the time and space necessary to nourish fidelity, the fulfillment is temporary and increases the tension and emptiness.

Acting only for pleasure is never healthy, sometimes unhealthy, and always immature. Behaving simply as physical beings is not whole or healthy. Nevertheless, satisfaction and pleasure can and should be part of healthy sexual relations. Integrated with committed (faithful) love, the physical pleasure of sex is enriched and deepened—and the love is intensified, concretized, and nourished.

Escape

Another motive for genital sex is to escape painful feelings. For example, some people want to escape from loneliness. Although this is very human and understandable, it does not work. Loneliness is seeking love, not primarily sex. The question of loneliness is "Will someone love me?" Sex without love or commitment is an inadequate answer.

A very lonely person with little self-worth might accept the counterfeit of love given in sexual gratification. When in the pits of boredom and loneliness, almost "any body" seems better than "no body." Sex can fulfill empty yearnings, but again, fulfillment is temporary and the activity soon impedes our growth in love.

Tension and boredom also can move a person toward genital behavior. As in the case of loneliness, sex can ease many discomforts. It may help us feel less empty and bored, more filled and excited. But again, these comfortable consequences are temporary; the irony is that they produce more boredom and tension later. It is better to listen to these feelings and seek healthier ways to respond to them, ways that will help us become more aware of and responsive to others.

Certainly pleasure, comfort, escape, and fulfillment can be positive benefits of healthy marital sex. To escape tension through marital sex can be a healthy way to receive needed comfort, to be energized, and to gain perspective on one's primary reason for being: love.

Nevertheless, a seductive feature of sex is to cause us to forget or escape the tensions of everyday living. It can move us out of our tense, everyday world and into an erotic and comfortable world. Faithful lovers, rather than using this ecstasy to escape from self, move out of the ordinary world to express and foster their love, so to cope better with everyday living.

Yearning to be whole

Genital sex can generate a feeling of being whole. "Wholeness" can especially attract those living fragmented or less than integral lives. To those who live a "heady" existence, a life "from the neck up," sex can be a way of affirming the rest of the self—especially that "from the neck down." A "thinkaholic," someone who operates from the neck up and sees truth coming only from rational thought, may engage periodically in sex as a way of becoming whole and embodied.

One expression of the longing for wholeness is a striving for self-completion. A man and a woman can complement each other in sexual relations. A man finds "his other half" in a woman, and she in him. Through committed love, a couple becomes one with each other and, paradoxically, each becomes more of himself or herself. By giving, surrendering, and ultimately becoming helpless, one receives the gift of becoming wholly one—the basis of power.

However, if one uses another to affirm a shaky sexual identity, the sexual union can be unhealthy or at least immature. This form of "sex exploitation" may give the illusion of being what the individual is not—a mature person. Consider the example of a man who brags about being a "man" because of his sexual experiences. It is questionable that he is much of a man; he is more likely a "playboy"—a little, insecure person who likes to play. Like a child who plays with toys, the man plays with people in a sad attempt to convince himself and others that he is a complete man. The fact is that one does not find one's identity through mere genital sex; in fact, such experience hinders us.

A desire to be special

Genital sex is special and it can make us feel special. The unity of transcendent love and sensual pleasure, the ecstatic escape and intimate union, the naked I and thou, the creative power and helplessness, the comforting security and vulnerability, the invigorating fun and rest—these are some of the many paradoxes. Genital sexuality's sacred sensuality calls for a privacy that proclaims a public love. Healthy, loving sex is very special. It ought to be celebrated, for it is a sacred (*kairos*) time.

Power

Genital sex is powerful. It can create, procreate, transcend, give pleasure, comfort, heal, humor, and unite. It can give and receive, evoke vulnerability and helplessness, provide the security to share oneself, and show or give hints of one's best self. Indeed, other forms of love can be just as or more powerful than genital love; nevertheless, genital sex has much to offer.

Some forms of power are less than healthy. The power of love and of being one with and for each other differs significantly from the power of manipulation and exploitation. Manipulation involves handling people as if they were objects to be controlled for one's own benefit rather than persons to be respected. Likewise, exploitation refers to using others for general gain. Seducing another with dress or words, taking advantage of an innocent person, or making false promises are power plays intended to manipulate and exploit.

Sex can be used to control and conquer, especially when one feels inferior. The man who feels inferior to or threatened by women may use sex to put women "down" and to give himself the feeling of being "up." A woman mistreated by men may use sex to get even with them—she might, for example, excite men and then withdraw or ridicule them.

Hostility under the guise of love can be a powerful drive for genital relations. Some men treat women as second-class citizens or as objects to use for their own satisfaction. They regard a woman as the enemy, someone to use, lower, or hurt. Many men, failing to acknowledge how women have influenced and/or controlled their lives, harbor hidden fear and resentment. These men are disposed to keep women "lower" and "down" as a way of dealing with their insecurity. Acting from hostility is never good or healthy.

The comments of this man betray such an inclination: "Yea, I scored last week. You know, chicks are made for men. They're like buses: you get on and you get off. There's nothing like making a broad and balling. What else are women good for? Yea. And there are plenty around who want to play." Underlying this man's crude language, which more aptly describes an athletic contest than love, is inferiority and hostility. He certainly is not the man he pretends to be.

Past experiences

Past experiences can impede or encourage us. For example, a boy very dependent on his mother may pursue women who mother him when he becomes an adult. Or a man who has been hurt somehow by a woman can learn to fear and hate women, unknowingly trying to dominate them sexually to deal with his insecurity and to express his hate. Rape is a significant example of this. Likewise, a woman who idolizes her father may idolize men (or marry one) who is like her father. If she has been abused by a man, she might display her resentment by using sex to manipulate and dominate men. A codependent woman (or man) may submit to violence in a futile attempt to resolve past problems.

Some people yearn to be intimate because they have never experienced intimacy with anyone on any level—including parents and friends. They transform their basic need to be loved into a quest for genital intimacy. What they really want and need— acceptance, affirmation, and love—they do not get. Although the pain of loneliness is lessened temporarily through genital sex, they soon feel more lonely and more frustrated. Genital sex is simply an inadequate response to the fact of past deprivation. What we are looking for deep within ourselves is more permanent than immediate gratification. What everyone needs is an experience that fosters permanent growth in love.

Here is the testimony of a woman who had little affection from anyone, including her parents, and is starved for affection: "No, I'm not proud of myself. I know I have the reputation of being an easy lay. Every man I go out with is prepared for one thing: screwing me. But nobody understands. I don't want to be screwed; I simply want to be loved. I feel ashamed. I guess I'm sometimes desperate enough to do almost anything for a little affection."

It is important to realize that our past can also help us. Healthy sex (primary, affective, and genital) education and experience in childhood and adolescence serve as the foundations for healthy, adult sexuality. Observing healthy marital and sexual models highly influences one's sexual future. Growing up with responsible, good parents who are passionately in love has a positive impact. Emphatically, the past plays a crucial role in our present and future sexual lives.

There is an axiom in sexology that if you don't use it (sex), you'll lose it—the practice of sexuality increases the likelihood of better sex. If one has a consistent and healthy sex life, sex will get better as one ages. In time, one will learn not only better techniques but also how to be more sensitive, gentle, sharing, and loving—how to give as well as how to receive more pleasure and fulfillment. As in most things, improvement comes through knowledge and practice.

In the course of years, a married couple can build a storehouse of rich and rewarding memories that they can share and enjoy. Past experiences serve to enrich the present even without consciously calling them forth. The more we "know" each other, the better our lives will be.

CHAPTER 6

Nonhealthy Ways to Cope

Although each of us experiences varying degrees of genital desire according to constitution, learning, situation, stage and kind of development, all of us do have genital feelings. To be human is also to be genital. Throughout our lives, we yearn at various times to be genitally intimate. This desire can be frustrating and confusing if gratification is incomplete or not forthcoming. We may feel we are missing something significant. Wanting to be loved and to give love sexually is a natural longing.

In the next two chapters, we will explore and analyze four basic ways of dealing with genitality: negative defense mechanisms, gratification, positive coping mechanisms, and integration. These ways of dealing with sex involve conscious or unconscious processes and value choices. This chapter considers negative defense mechanisms and physical gratification— common but nonhealthy ways of reacting to genital desire.

Negative defense mechanisms

Negative defense mechanisms are processes by which we protect ourselves against unpleasant or anxious feelings that tend to expose unacceptable parts of ourselves. When we use negative defense mechanisms, we are rejecting certain aspects of ourselves—admitting such experiences would evoke unacceptable pain. Defenses are usually unconscious; we do not consciously or willfully choose to use them. Early in life, we may learn to take a less than honest look at our sexual feelings. The good news is that since it is unlikely such defenses are instinctual or innate, they can be unlearned. We have the capacity openly to face our sexual self.

Defense mechanisms are common. Some psychologists suggest that everyone uses them to some extent; they are necessary to survive. Ideally, we would wish to avoid employing negative defense mechanisms. Realistically, most of us at some time use them. However, how frequently, why, and how we use them highly influence healthy living. The challenge is to become aware of defense mechanisms and to be freed for healthy living.

Defenses distort one's perception of reality. The more they are used, the more reality is filtered and biased. They close us to experiences, thereby decreasing freedom and creative control of life as well as impeding personal and interpersonal communication. Furthermore, defenses tend to be self-reinforcing. The more we use them, the easier it becomes and the more difficult it is to change.

Defenses exact a price. They cause us to waste much time and energy in nonproductive and repetitious behavior—in trying to be what and who we are not. Moreover, defenses are not only painful to oneself; often, they are irritating and harmful to others. When we use them, we are more likely to manipulate others to satisfy our needs and less likely to be sufficiently flexible and open to understand and care for others.

A primary reason for using defense mechanisms is to ward off anxiety resulting from unacceptable experiences. For instance, we may defend against genital feelings because we become anxious, ashamed, or guilty when we feel sexual: sexual feelings evoke unpleasantness which we hope to avoid. However, although immediate unpleasantness may be reduced, we violate ourselves by rejecting an essential part of our personhood. Defense mechanisms are self-defeating. We achieve short-term gains in the reduction of pain and the production of pleasure, but our long-term losses are much greater and debilitating.

Repression

Repression is a defense mechanism that often pervades many other defense mechanisms. In fact, many defenses are based on repression. Repression is an unconscious effort to exclude certain experiences from conscious awareness. We fool ourselves by not being consciously aware of being unaware. We still feel sexual but refuse to admit to our genital feelings. We pretend not to be pretending. Confusing? Yes. This is why persons who constantly repress live in a world of make-believe.

Consider, for example, a person who represses genital feelings. She (or he) does not choose consciously to lie to herself, for her repression is primarily an unconscious process. Although she may have some anxious moments of questioning her sexual self, seldom can she allow herself to reflect on her genitality. If one tells her that she represses, she will feel threatened and consequently become even more defensive. She may innocently deny, anxiously withdraw, vehemently protest, or sincerely intellectualize the truth. Whatever she does, she does not accept and affirm her sexual self.

Why do we unconsciously and automatically expunge experiences from conscious and free awareness? Usually, it is because we have learned and relearned that certain experiences are "unacceptable," make no sense, or are bad in themselves, and that "no good person" would experience them. We can learn early in life that to maintain self-esteem or to be a "loved me," certain experiences must be repressed. To admit such feelings would risk rejection from others or evoke unhealthy guilt (self-rejection).

Consider the repressed woman as a child. If her parents constantly fostered repression of sex, punishing any sexual expression or discussion, she could learn to feel that her self-esteem depends on being asexual and thus feel compelled to repress her sexuality. When sex suddenly and strongly emerges in adolescence, she finds herself poorly prepared to integrate it. After all, she learned to feel that being a good person means being nonsexual. Moreover, her sexual repression may restrict other opportunities for growth. Solitude, for instance, essential to healthy growth, might be minimized or filled with noisy thoughts to escape the silence that could pressure her to listen to what she does not want to hear: the voice of her sexuality.

Here are the comments of a man, also a victim of repression: "I can't stand to be alone. I get these uncomfortable feelings. Yea, I get sexually aroused along with thoughts and fantasies. Then I feel impure and sinful. I don't know what to do. Why me? I try so hard to be pure—to have no sexual feelings and thoughts. But it seems the more I try, the worse it gets."

Repression is costly. When we categorically reject a part of who we are, we pay a price. Repression is a negative reinforcement: what actually happens is that instead of getting rid of an experience, repression increases its strength and promotes pressure for expression. Many costly behaviors come with repressed sexual energy. We may become frustrated, irritable, or angry. We may withdraw from intimacy for fear of being sexually aroused, and perhaps use false notions of chastity and celibacy to rationalize our avoidance. We might project or displace our feelings by blaming others for being unchaste, or perhaps achieve some vicarious satisfaction and shaky self-reinforcement by becoming the community or family "sex censor."

Whatever happens, we simply waste time and energy in trying to be what we are not. We become exhausted from going against our natural self. Our freedom is curtailed and our life is violated. Indeed, absolute repression of sexuality is unchaste because it is impure and disrespectful to self and others. Such repression denies human embodiment and makes us "spiritual prunes"—dry and inert.

Denial

Denial is perhaps the most blatant and primitive defense mechanism. It occurs when we refuse to admit that obvious facts or actions exist. In contrast to repression, denial often deals with external interpersonal and environmental activities more than internal (intrapsychic) processes. Denial is rejection of evidence that is obvious to almost anyone except the denying person. A common example is the alcoholic (and often his or her family), who denies this serious disease even when he or she is drunk. An example in the context of sexuality is a woman who dresses and speaks in a sexually provocative manner, and yet completely denies the obvious evidence. Another is a man who treats women as sex objects and flirts with them, yet denies manifestations of sexual exploitation when confronted with them. People who deny use primitive defense mechanisms because they refuse to admit clear evidence. Like all negative defenses, denial is an unconscious process. Confronting denying persons threatens them and often evokes more denial.

Denial often will include more than one person. Such collusion means that two or more people, without consciously agreeing, deny the same reality. For example, a man and a woman do not admit they are sexually attracted to each other, sensing that such feelings are unacceptable and/or too much to cope with. Not only do many people deny the same reality; they also pretend that they are not pretending. Spousal, family, friend, or community collusion only exacerbates and worsens (enables) the reality. Consider the case of a couple who deny their daughter's (or son's) promiscuity. Denying to themselves and each other enables the daughter to continue her sexual activity. More importantly, this denial precludes any offer to her of healthy alternatives.

Rationalization

Rationalization is an irrational way of using rationality. Rationalization is used when one cannot confront the real issue and so attempts to explain and justify feelings or behavior with impersonal, socially acceptable reasons. Instead of taking responsibility for acts, the rationalizer tries to minimize their possible effects or to justify his or her actions. The rationalizer might say, for instance, that almost everyone has premarital or extramarital experiences—why shouldn't I? As rationalizers, we try to hide behind a general statement instead of reflecting on the true healthiness and/or holiness of our actions. We might say that everything works out in the long run anyhow, so why worry or think about it. We might say that as long as we are sincere and honest, our sexual intimacy is okay. Rationalizers fail to realize that sincerity and honesty do not necessarily guarantee health.

People who rationalize sex often try to fool themselves about the effects of genital involvement. Take the example of a nonmarried couple who engage in intercourse. They rationalize their genital involvement, saying that any act done in love is okay. They forget or repress the fact that care should be a committed and responsible love expressed in the proper time and space. They justify their genital intimacy with a nonhealthy theory of care.

Fantasy

Although fantasy can be healthy, it is not so when it becomes more important than reality. Fantasies are seductive; they offer the illusion of intimate fulfillment without risk, responsibility, or limits. Fantasy can be creative—and it can fool us.

Consider the example of a man who nurtures many genital fantasies, seldom approaches people in reality, and fails to make healthy sense of his genitality. Although he feels inferior to women, his compulsive fantasy of overpowering women serves to overcompensate for his poor sexual identity and self-esteem. Instead of running from reality and hiding in fantasy, he would do better to understand and learn from his true feelings.

Insulation

Insulation occurs when we protect ourselves against hurt and disappointment by not allowing ourselves to care very much. Such "emotional blunting" enables us to remain uninvolved. Instead of being warm and approachable, we keep cool and distant to protect ourselves from emotional and sexual involvement. Insulated persons may not be stimulated genitally or put themselves in situations where this may occur, but they pay the price by being cold and lifeless.

Those who emotionally insulate themselves tend to love "from the neck up." Even though they may be quite competent mentally, their emotional expression is restricted and curtailed. Being unable to express care highly constricts one's life and love.

A woman made the following comments about her husband: "My husband is a good person. I can trust and count on him; he will do anything for me. But he simply cannot share himself. He seems so detached and cold, especially when I ask him how he feels. Even in sex, which is becoming less frequent, he hides. He seems interested only in genital gratification, not in intimacy."

This man may have learned that expressing feelings, including sexual ones, is unmanly, unacceptable, dangerous, or unnecessary. Whatever the reason, he has learned to cope with his feelings by being detached and insulated. It is sad because he is a good person, but a serious consequence of his insulation is that he is losing the art of caring—and is losing his wife. Being boxed in, he will suffocate and lose his spirit. Furthermore, his genital life will continue to dissipate because such intimacy needs the expression of love to grow.

Isolation

A similar technique is isolation: cutting oneself off from sexual situations that produce stress. To withdraw freely from a situation can be healthy, but to be compelled to withdraw from any sexually stimulating situation is not healthy.

Let's take the example of a man who withdraws from women because such involvement evokes sexual feelings. He constantly censors situations and sees only the possible bad. In playing "safe" he seldom goes anywhere to have fun and make heterosocial contact, fearing sexual stimulation. Instead of facing and making sense of his sexual feelings, he isolates himself.

Internal isolation or dissociation involves the separating of values from activities: actions do not fit words. A man who professes chastity while being sexist is separating theory from practice. The woman who claims sexual openness but refuses to discuss sexual issues is doing the same. The man who preaches love but is afraid of intimacy lives out of his head, not his experience. These individuals fool themselves and often others, thinking and verbalizing one philosophy while living another.

Regression

Regression describes the tendency to revert to activities—thought, judgment, and behavior—that were characteristic of one's earlier development. When a situation becomes too threatening or overwhelming, we regress to a level at which we have little or no responsibility or to a time when we felt more secure.

For instance, we can regress to (pregenital) childhood because there we feel relatively "sexless" and less responsible. An example of this is a woman whose father sexually abused her. Besides repressing her painful feelings, she is anorexic—an attempt to be disembodied and formless so that any evidence of sexuality will "disappear." Furthermore, she dresses to look like a little girl instead of a mature, sexual woman. By denying her sexuality and regressing to prepuberty, she manages to ward off acknowledgement of her painful past. However, the price she pays includes physiological disturbances, lack of intimacy, failure to manifest herself, and overall frustration and debilitation.

However, some regressive behavior can be healthy. Giggling

and kidding about sex, for instance, may be a pleasant way to return to the past, a fun way to explore new feelings. Regression as a change of pace or a temporary growth period, not a constant way of coping with sex, can be healthy. A husband and wife may take delight occasionally in teasing each other as if they were younger than they really are. A group of friends may regress to adolescence in joking about sexuality. However, people who too often regress to adolescence foster immaturity rather than wholesome fun.

Projection

Blaming others for what we think, feel, or do is projection. This defense mechanism maintains self-esteem and adequacy by placing on others our own unacceptable feelings and impulses. We may accuse others of being unchaste and manipulative in their intentions as a way of dealing with our own unchaste and manipulative feelings. This can be difficult for the people we accuse; often they do not know what is occurring. When they are so accused, they may feel guilty for feelings they do not even have, or may become confused and angry with us. If we are domineering, we can make an innocent and often dependent person feel guilty while preserving the perception of our own innocence.

Placing blame on other people or events violates both our own and others' sexuality. Consider, for example, a repressed woman who gets drunk at a party. Under the influence of alcohol, she engages in genital relations. The next morning she uses projection, placing the blame on the alcohol or on the man, or on both. She does not accept her own responsibility. This projection enables her to maintain her sense of chastity. Consequently, she retains some degree of self-esteem as a "pure" and guiltless person.

Besides being a matter of dishonesty with oneself, blaming others prevents personal growth. If others are the reasons for our actions, our freedom to change is highly impaired. We imply that others or events must change in order for us to change. Even if others are at fault, we should never base our freedom to grow on others. After all, they may never change. Besides, we may invest too much time and energy futilely trying to change others rather than ourselves. Although we do have impact on and influence others positively and negatively—and we can *help* others to change—we cannot in fact change them. We can change only our own life, hopefully with the help of others and God.

Displacement

Displacement is the switching of emotional expressions from the eliciting person to some other, less risky person or object. For example, instead of expressing anger toward the superior who occasioned it, we unreflectively dump it on a less threatening person—a spouse, a friend, a child, a stranger. Instead of actively confronting the boss, we yell at the innocent checkout clerk, or drive home recklessly, hollering at anyone in our way.

Displacement is the transferring of emotions from an appropriate person to a less threatening person. Some people build up through ongoing repression a "slush fund" of emotion. Then, suddenly, they "dump it" on a relatively "safe" person. A man who represses sexuality might build up a slush fund of sexual desires which he periodically displaces (and satisfies) with a prostitute or with masturbation. He momentarily decreases his sexual tension, but fails to deal with his sexuality in a healthy way.

Overcompensation

A subtle mode of defending oneself against sexuality is overcompensating. Basically, this means overreacting to certain feelings. Some people engage frequently in genital behavior to make up for feelings of sexual inferiority. So-called liberated swingers, they try futilely to gain a sense of sexual identity, but only increase their sense of inadequacy. Such individuals can be deceptive because on the surface they look open and free. Actually, they feel inferior and are too afraid to risk the surrender love requires. Overcompensation is a mask that covers and hides the whole self rather than uncovering and sharing it.

Men particularly are prone to overcompensate for their lack of authentic sexuality by engaging in genital promiscuity. They are often programmed to be the vanguards of genitality, to feel that they can find true identity in genital conquests. Unfortunately, increasingly more women are following this mad male model of sexual liberation.

Reaction formation

Another subtle tactic for dealing with sexuality is reaction formation. This approach replaces unacceptable urges (sexuality) with completely opposite behaviors and oftentimes correspondingly intolerant attitudes. Whenever one goes to an extreme, one feels the opposite extreme within. For example, sexual prudes often are highly sexual. People all too willing to condemn others' sexual activities may get satisfaction from this censoring. Reaction formations have the advantage of allowing one to maintain a questionable self-concept of being healthy while at the same time having nonhealthy satisfaction.

Some people try to lead celibate lives because they are afraid to face their sexual desires. They equate celibacy with being nongenital; they practice celibacy as a way of coping with unacceptable genital feelings. Such celibacy can also be supported by the culture—everybody likes "good" people. This does not mean that all celibates employ reaction formations against genitality. Overall, vowed celibates (sisters, brothers, and priests) are probably at least as healthy as noncelibates.

Undoing

Undoing is used by people who tend to be perfectionistic, scrupulous, and prone to guilt. A scrupulous person obsessed with the sinfulness of feelings and fantasies usually identifies feelings with acts. He or she assumes that feeling sexual is the same as behaving sexually. Since such a person has sexual feelings, guilt is intense and frequent. A scrupulous person can waste enormous amounts of time and energy trying to undo guilt evoked by natural feelings through confession and penance. This individual feels compelled to go through rituals like saying a set of prayers perfectly until he has absolutely cleaned his "moral slate." Instead of helping the sufferer to face and integrate sexuality, the compulsive rituals of undoing only bury and exacerbate it. Soon the submerged sexuality emerges and the corresponding compulsive activities are again triggered. The scrupulous person tries to be what he or she is not: nonsexual.

When we genuinely violate sexuality, we should feel guilty—but not primarily because of transgressing a law. We should feel guilty for using oneself and/or another. The practice of undoing usually rises from guilt that occurs from breaking unrealistic laws and/or from an erroneous conscience. This ritual of atonement is not healthy because it does not deal directly with sexuality. Moreover, it comes from a compulsive or unfree will. True "at-one-ment" suggests that we become one with ourselves and with one another. It is the opposite of alienation from self and others.

Sympathism

Sympathism is the practice of trying to get others to feel sorry for us and to support us. A woman who feels overwhelmed by sexual feelings and unconsciously feels helpless in dealing with them may employ sympathism. She tries to run from sexual awareness by complaining constantly of her problems. She manipulates people's compassion so she can indulge herself in their sympathy and hide from sexual awareness.

Sympathism can be a subtle defense; people believe such a person has no sexual problems or does not think of sexuality— how could a suffering and sick person be sexual? Complaints, however, usually and quickly turn people off so that the complainers are left with themselves and their sexuality. These people are then compelled to become even "sicker" to pressure others to help them run from sexual awareness. The therapeutic challenge is to see through this sincere sympathism to the underlying sexual repression.

Acting out

Acting out is another defense mechanism that, because it is actually a gratification of needs, may not seem so defensive. Acting out refers to the process of dispelling and reducing pressure by acting in a nonhealthy manner. Some people who repress genital desires go on periodic sprees of sexual fantasy, pornographic reading, masturbation, or sexual intercourse. They may seldom gratify their repressed sexuality, but several times a year they act out interpersonally and/or alone.

For some, acting out seems to reduce genital tension and even evoke guilt that temporarily controls genital behavior for the immediate future. They get genital desires "out of their system" until they build up again. Acting out is not healthy; it focuses on impulsive or compulsive gratification that is often due to compulsive building up of sexual tension.

The experience expressed by this man bears this out: "I try so hard and yet I always seem to fail. I really try to keep out any sexual feeling and thoughts, and things seem to be okay for weeks and sometimes even months. But then, bang! I lose all control and I go on a rampage of gratification. Why does this happen to me?" This well-intentioned man is probably repressing his sexuality and thereby inadvertently building up pressure to satisfy himself.

Gratification

We can satisfy genital needs directly; this is tempting for many reasons. If we are tense, lonely, or bored, sexual satisfaction seems to take all this away. Indeed it can, but only temporarily. It can make us feel like something, someone, somebody who is fulfilled. It can purge discomfort and give a feeling of peace.

Also, we can engage in genital behavior to evoke pleasure. However, pursuing only pleasure can be unhealthy, or at least "not healthy"—that is, while seeking pleasure is "normal," as an isolated endeavor it does not foster wholistic growth. This so-called normal, physical emphasis in sex is mad and bad because it treats self and others as simply physical genital beings; this violates personal integrity. To identify the human person as merely genital is to debase our own and the other's dignity. Genitality must be integrated into the total person.

Finally, we have noted that single life, unlike marital life, lacks the commitment, time, and place necessary to foster healthy sexual growth. Since genital sexuality calls for marital commitment, single people who engage in genital relations can eventually feel cheated, frustrated, tense, unfulfilled, or resentful when the promise of love is not kept. Of course, married persons who do not nurture their commitment can feel just as hurt and empty—often more so.

Unfortunately, extramarital sex can be considered "normal" in that such behavior is frequently practiced and socially accepted or tolerated; it may also reduce tension and afford pleasure. But, mores are not the same as morals. Extramarital relations are neither healthy nor good.

Certainly, all extramarital sex is not primarily or exclusively selfish. It can be a sincere expression of love that is centered on another. When two persons are in love, they truly (without exploitation) desire the union and life that genital sex offers. It is difficult to abstain from genital relations when authentic love pervades the relationship.

Nevertheless, the challenge is to abstain from genital involvement while fostering love. Although abstinence can be frustrating and even seem unnatural, it is best. As we have seen, extramarital lovemaking will not promote love; the marital commitment, time, and place necessary for spontaneous and healthy genital sex are missing. Although premarital and extramarital genital behavior can have meaning, they remain nonhealthy because they impede ongoing psychological and spiritual growth. If this is true, what can we do with our sexual desires whether they include or exclude love?

CHAPTER 7

Healthy Ways to Cope and Integrate

Many of us learn only two ways of dealing with sexual desires: repression or gratification. This is not much of a choice; we have seen that both coping mechanisms fall short of being healthy, particularly for nonmarried persons.

There are healthy ways to cope with and integrate sexuality. They apply to both nonmarried and married persons. Certain psychological strategies reduce stress, increase freedom and control, and consequently facilitate healthy growth. Certain spiritual strategies help us to deal with, integrate, and enjoy sexuality. We will consider the psychological approaches first.

Suppression

Suppression, like repression, is the checking of an experience. Suppression, unlike repression, involves conscious or free awareness of an experience that is kept from overt expression. Suppression is a "no" that is based on a more fundamental "yes."

When we choose to suppress sexuality, we begin by freely affirming feelings and sexual desires, deciding not to promote or act on them. Instead of being an unfree and unconscious act, suppression is a free and often conscious decision. Instead of living in repression's world of pretense, we claim and affirm our sexuality, freely choosing to control our genital behavior. While repression involves self-rejection and negation, suppression uses self-affirmation and free choice which promote healthy living.

Ideally, we should admit all experiences to ourselves, if not necessarily expressing them to others or acting on them. When we feel sexual, we can admit and affirm that experience. Acceptance, in contrast to repression, increases the alternatives for more healthy behavior.

To suspend or bracket thoughts and feelings is one alternative. For instance, suspending genital feelings is appropriate while listening, studying, teaching, or performing a task; it provides the discipline needed to focus freely on the matter at hand without disruptions. Having neither the desire nor the time to reflect on genital feelings, they are bracketed, put on the shelf. In the circumstance that we urgently desire genital expression, it may not be a good time for oneself or the other, an appropriate place may not be available, or the commitment may be absent. In this case, we say "yes" to the feelings, then choose not to focus on them. We refuse to give them attention, thereby lessening their strength. (Attention, especially obsessive attention, usually reinforces feelings.)

Suppression is sometimes easy, at other times it is difficult. One's psychological state highly influences the degree of ease or difficulty. Someone who is lonely, sexually desirous, tired, and stressed will have more difficulty using suppression than one who feels connected, alert, comfortable, and without genital urges. Sometimes mortification and always discipline are necessary.

Mortification

The word mortification immediately evokes negative reactions. To many people, mortification elicits visions of painful and meaningless penance, self-punishment, or pathological asceticism. However, mortification is necessary sometimes for suppression and overall health as well. Mortification also is a "no" in service of a "yes." Meaning "to make dead," mortification is healthy when it fosters growth. Healthy mortification suggests that sometimes death is necessary in order to have life.

Consider this scene: a man desires genital relations with his fiancée but freely chooses to mortify his feelings. He first affirms his genital feelings, then says "no" or mortifies the genital expression of his love. Instead of withdrawing from himself and his beloved, he rejects genital expression but remains present, with his desires, to his future wife. He remains sexual, but freely refuses to engage in any genital behavior. This man says, "Yes, I want very much to express my love in genital relations, but I do not think it would be best for either of us at this time." Such mortification can be very difficult and uncomfortable, but it is a "death" that promotes a life of love.

Mortification may seem old-fashioned or masochistic, but it is quite congruent with contemporary research on life-cycle development and spiritual formation. Although the word mortification is not used, most developmental psychologists readily agree that growth periodically involves pain and the letting go of both negative and positive experiences. Classical and contemporary spirituality also affirm the need to purge both negative and positive experiences (e.g., to move from one level of development to another). Mortification is not outdated; it is a necessary approach to wholistic growth.

Discipline

Suppression and mortification demand discipline. Although discipline is usually equated with rigidity, it is rather the basis of freedom. Many people find discipline difficult because in childhood they had almost all their needs satisfied. Moreover, our culture promotes immediate satisfaction instead of delayed gratification. The person who has always gotten anything he or she wanted (food, TV, movies, toys, money, etc.) may find it more difficult to suppress sex than a person who did not have needs satisfied so readily. Discipline begins in early childhood. To embrace it later in life is difficult, but still possible. Lack of discipline leads to sexual license: doing whatever we want.

Discipline is both popular and unpopular today. On the one hand, discipline is glorified as the necessary condition for physical well-being, intellectual and career development, and spiritual growth. On the other hand, mass media, culture, and some individuals promote immediate gratification and a general flight from pain. Living for the moment or the most comfortable situation is the message. Such a philosophy and psychology encourages individualistic self-gratification.

As embodied persons, our freedom is both limited and dynamic. Responding to the realities of time, space, genetics, anatomy, physiology, culture, education, environment, religion, and other factors, discipline molds—limits and facilitates—our abilities and behavior. It controls and hones our embodiment to enable us to express ourselves as freely as possible. Without discipline, an individual will easily succumb to immediate gratification or to sexist and hedonistic scripts provided by the culture and people within it. Discipline helps us to control and abstain from forces that impede free choice.

From repression to suppression

Problems can emerge when one moves from repression to suppression. During this transitional time, a person may act in a way almost the opposite of past repressive behavior. For example, consider a woman who repressed her sexual feelings in early adolescence and young adulthood. In her thirties or later she becomes conscious of and has opportunities for sexual involvement. After many years, she now suddenly finds herself confronted with intense genital desires and fantasies. Confused and fascinated with her newly emergent genital self, she feels pressured to act. Instead of being defensive about or unaware of sex, she shows flexibility and vitality, thinks about and wants to talk about sex, and is tempted to experiment with her new feelings. Since her friends have been used to her old "sexless" self, the woman's new sexual self conflicts with their expectations. Some of them may pressure her to be her old self, criticizing her, asking her what is wrong, alienating her. The others may encourage her to gratify her desires, steering her toward situations where genital gratification can occur. All of these people err. They would do better making themselves available to help her accept and take time to learn healthy ways to cope with her changing self.

Sublimation

Sublimation, meaning to raise or to elevate feelings, refers to the redirecting of energy from one activity to another that is judged to be culturally, socially, physically, functionally, aesthetically, or spiritually "higher" or better. Sublimation, like suppression, is an acceptance of feelings that we choose not to gratify in behavior. Rather than holding feelings in check as with suppression, the one who sublimates rechannels or invests energy into an activity that is in harmony with his or her values. Of course, if one has immature or unhealthy values, sublimation as well as suppression will be difficult or seem senseless.

Sublimation is a frequently encouraged approach to dealing with genital desires. Instead of directly satisfying genital desires, this tactic invests genital energy in activities that are congruent with and promote healthy and good living. This approach serves well for both single and married persons. Married persons, after all, cannot and should not satisfy themselves every time they feel genital desire.

Sublimation begins by suppressing sexual feelings (which means affirming and controlling them), then freely choosing to direct our energy toward actions that promote healthy living. A frequently used approach in the past was to "get busy," especially in manual labor or athletics. This kind of simple sublimation is still useful and helpful but there are other ways also. For example, we can rechannel our sexual energy into intellectual pursuits such as studying and reading, or direct it toward aesthetic and creative activity. When suppressed and invested in love, sublimated sexuality can promote healthy relationships. Indeed, it is possible to sublimate genital sex while remaining in and promoting a relationship of love. With the discipline of practice and time, sublimation can become largely habitual.

One woman describes her use of sublimation: "When I feel real sexual, I can do several things. Sometimes I clean my room; at other times, I just get involved in a book or a TV program. When it's really intense, I do some strenuous activity like running or cleaning my apartment. I find that calling a friend helps, too."

Anticipation

Anticipation can maintain and foster healthy sexuality. This refers to the practice of predicting what is likely to occur. As its etymology indicates, anticipation suggests that one foresees what will probably happen and plans a course of action that will prevent negative consequences.

For instance, a single woman may know that at certain times during her monthly cycle she will be more lonely and will need more affection, affirmation, and understanding. She also knows from her past experience that when she drinks alcohol and/or is tired, she has less control and is more vulnerable to satisfying her sexual desires. She knows that, given these conditions and others, she must take special care of herself. Consequently, accepting a dinner invitation from a charming and sexually manipulative man at his apartment would be foolish if she wants to avoid sexual involvement. Likewise, an engaged couple who feel vulnerable must take extra precautions—both individually and together—to safeguard chastity. They know what can occur.

Effective anticipation depends on knowing oneself: How do I feel now? How have I (and others) acted in past situations like this? Instead of falling into negative defense mechanisms, this questioning helps us to openly accept and to learn from our present feelings and past experiences, which promises a better future. Perfect judgments and correct courses of action are not guaranteed, but self-awareness and learning does increase significantly one's freedom of choice.

Anticipation is one way to cope with and change the problem of compulsive masturbation. For instance, knowing the times of the month and day when one is more vulnerable can be helpful. Alcoholics Anonymous has an acronym called HALT. It is a reminder that when one is *H*ungry (in whatever way), *A*ngry, *L*onely, or *T*ired, it is time to be careful. This advice is relevant not only to alcoholism but to any problem. Indeed, we must halt sometimes: stop, step back, think, and take measures to deal with our vulnerability.

Implicit in the strategy of anticipation is humility—the acceptance of being on earth and of being less than completely free. Humility is the recognition that we are neither in perfect control nor can we orchestrate all feelings and behaviors in ourself or others. This recognition leads to serenity. Feelings come and go in frequency and intensity; sometimes hormones seem to have a life of their own. But we can take measures to exercise choice and control within our limitations. Being humble does not mean putting ourselves down or being weak; rather, it is lifting ourselves up to self-awareness and being strong in loving self-control.

People who think they can always control their feelings and behaviors and/or handle those of others are fools. They deceive themselves, assuming they have more power than the facts bear out. Such self-deception is often rationalization for unacceptable behavior. Consider, for example, a celibate man in love with a woman. If he thinks he can spend considerable personal time with her without being moved to physical intimacy, he is arrogant or naive. Such pride will only lead to trouble. This is not to suggest that he be paranoid, withdrawn, or fearful. He should just be humble in accepting that he cannot control everything. He should anticipate situations when and where he or she will be vulnerable and plan to use healthy coping strategies: suppression, detachment, integration.

Anticipation, of course, can be negative or unrealistic. Expecting the worst lays the foundation for self-fulfilling prophecies. Repression, low self-esteem, or a puritanical conscience engenders jaded, narrow expectations. Open acceptance, learning from one's internal and external reality—these lead to a vital, humble, and serene approach to life. Positive anticipation presupposes and fosters the wisdom and courage that engender healthy sexuality.

Friends

Friends and other trustworthy persons can be helpful in coping with and resolving long- or short-term crises. Disclosure— sharing our sexual feelings and dilemmas with a friend—can help in many ways. First, being genuinely listened to and understood invariably increases well-being. Second, getting our inside feelings out decreases stress, conserves energy, and increases hope and freedom. Moreover, we feel less unique and alone by sharing; we discover that the boat we are on is not empty but very crowded. Instead of being self-dependent and isolated, we become one with others; instead of feeling alien, we realize we are decidedly human.

"For some time, I've had these sexual desires and fantasies," comments one woman. "I sort of knew that it was okay, and yet I felt frustrated, confused, and alone. Although I knew better, I still felt that few people felt like I did, or that no one would understand, or that I would be criticized for being weird or wrong. Finally, after mustering the courage to share with an older friend, I felt more human and at peace. Even though she didn't say much, I felt normal, that I could work things out. I feel much better now."

When a mature friend is unavailable or the trust level in self or another is low, a counselor may help. A therapeutic context should offer confidentiality, security, acceptance, understanding, and the help to resolve and improve. If progress, which usually involves discomfort, is not discerned and experienced rather quickly, acquire a new therapist.

Another approach is to join a fellowship group. Many groups such as Alcoholics Anonymous and its many offshoots follow a wholistic approach. People with similar interests, problems, and challenges meet regularly to help one another within and outside the group meeting. Such compassionate and confrontational fellowships give support, courage, and suggestions for improvement.

With or without professional help, we can help one another. People who have or are going through similar experiences can help one another. It is not necessary to feel alone or discouraged; we can gain the courage and insight to change for the better.

As one woman noted about her group experience, "I never dreamed that so many people felt like I do. I thought no one could feel as confused and hurt as I. Then I listened to the stories and feelings of others in my group, how they managed to feel better, freer, okay. The group listened to my experiences of being sexually abused—they really understood. They gently and firmly helped me out of denial; they supported me as I expressed my anger and fear. Because of them I began to come out of my confusion and guilt. Having been there themselves, they gave me a special gift of empathy. And no, they didn't treat me with kid gloves, but they were compassionate and understanding. Now I am happy to say that I've accepted what happened to me, that I've forgiven my father and mother. What's more, I'm helping others to come out of their black holes and see and enjoy the light."

Integration

Genital sex, we have seen, has much more than a physical meaning; it can have a direct and positive influence on our psychological and spiritual life. Therefore, it should not be regarded as an enemy or impediment. We are challenged to experience sex as a friend, a help in living a healthy single or married life. Indeed, genital feelings can evoke and promote authentic personal integration.

The etymological meaning of integration—to make whole—gives an important clue to its sexual application, particularly in light of the wholistic perspective stressed here. Integration denotes the process of renewing or restoring an *integer*, a whole. Clinically, integration involves experiencing the whole from which the parts emerge. Integrating genital feelings begins by experiencing genitality as part of and a revelation of the whole person. While genital feelings, fantasies, and behavior are physical functions, they also manifest and reveal something about ourselves and others as integral (whole) people. Healthy people learn to experience the whole person partially revealed in genitality. If we overemphasize the genital, we fragment ourselves and the other.

Respect, meaning "to see again" or to take a second look, is a key to integration. Respectful persons understand genital sex as a manifestation of the whole person. Their creative seeing enables them to accept the invitation to appreciate the deeper dimensions of self and others. Instead of separating genital feelings from the whole self, or seeing them merely as biological functions, they experience sex as an invitation to wholeness.

"When I'm sexually attracted to a man, I make an effort not to focus only on sex," comments one woman. "I look at how he carries himself, speaks, and behaves. If I'm really interested, I try to find out about his personality, character, and values. I want to know how he thinks about important issues—and me as well. I want to know if he is a jerk or a real man. Of course, if I were not sexually attracted to him in the first place, I might have passed him by."

She is right. Our sexual feelings invite us to the process of integration. Sex might be characterized as a "rupture" in everyday life that breaks through the forgetfulness and busyness of normal living to help us respect and fully appreciate ourselves and others. Specifically, sex says: "Stop! Respect reality—take a second look at yourself and the other. Don't take people for granted." However, what we see depends on how we look. Attitudes codetermine the meaning of reality—and consequently how we feel and behave. For example, an artist employing his aesthetic perspective is less likely to regard a nude woman as a genital partner; he will see her aesthetically. His "aesthetic" eyes appreciate her whole being—physical, psychological, spiritual. His painting will try to capture the woman's beauty, uniqueness, personality, and spirit. If his painting is good, it will help viewers to deepen their appreciation of all women. Likewise, authentic single or married lovers are not apt to identify themselves or others with a physical part (breasts, legs, genitals) or a function (wife, friend, lover); rather, they are inclined to experience these parts and functions as expressions and affirmations of the whole human being. Such persons are authentically chaste—they can appreciate without selfishness, manipulation, or exploitation. A chaste posture is a pure one; it is a respectful and integral presence to reality.

We have noted, too, that sexuality is a relational process; it incorporates or seeks another person in relation to oneself. Sex takes us out of ourselves. Moreover, the way we relate sexually to others is contingent on personal self-respect. To appreciate another's wholeness is to affirm and manifest our own wholeness; a respectful awareness of another's integrity presupposes and fosters our own integrity. To experience one's own sexuality in a healthy way increases the likelihood of appreciating the wholeness of another.

Differences between men and women

In earlier chapters, I proposed that women are more disposed than men to seek a deeper satisfaction than the physical when they feel sexual. They place genital sex in the light of tenderness, affection, and care, and tend to respond more readily to the call for a permanent and faithful commitment. Nevertheless, men also can respond to the sacredness of genitality and be more sensitive and caring.

In Western culture, however, men are more likely than women to isolate genital desire in terms of satisfaction. When genital desire incites a man to "take a second look," his experience depends largely on his attitude toward women. If he experiences a woman as an object for sexual satisfaction, he will identify her with her physical being, minimize or deny her wholeness, and consequently long to use her for selfish satisfaction.

The following remarks represent an immature attitude toward women: "Personally, I'm a boob man. Breasts really turn me on. The bigger and firmer, the better. Of course I don't mind nice legs and rears either. A nice face helps, too. God knew what he was doing when he made breasts. They really turn me on." This man sees only the parts of a woman, not her whole person. His crass and arrogant attitude betrays his immaturity and lack of respect for women—as well as for himself.

A healthy stance

What is it like to be a man who is genitally attracted to a woman's breasts? What does he experience? Does he see only or primarily breasts? If so, his experience is neither healthy nor good—no such independent reality as "breasts" exist; only a person who has breasts. This man separates and represses the psychological and especially spiritual dimensions of the woman and of himself. Consequently, he impoverishes what she and he are and can be. He lacks respect for himself. Moreover, he diminishes his integrity by failing to appreciate sexuality (his own and another's) as an expression of the whole person.

Ironically, his genital desires could help him to appreciate her as a person—beautiful, intelligent, resourceful, assertive, a mystery to behold. The healthier stance for this man would be to regard the woman and himself psychologically and spiritually as well as physically. Instead of fragmenting her being—separating her breasts from her personhood or maximizing the meaning of physical sex—he could respect more integrally her breasts as expressions of her personhood, womanhood, femininity, beauty, life, nurturance, and care. He could allow her breasts to evoke an appreciation of her whole being. Relating as a whole human being, he would then own a sexuality that is healthy and good.

Fantasies

Let us consider sexual fantasies in the light of integration. A woman may discover herself thinking or dreaming about genital sex. What does she experience? Does she imagine making love without weight, smell, touch, taste—a "senseless" love? Does she focus on genitals apart from the person, or on a person with genitals? How real is her sexual fantasy? Does she fantasize lovemaking as one euphoric state without limits, fears, and clumsiness? Does she want the pleasure of sex and the perfection of

93

intimacy without the limits and responsibilities of real, committed sex? Her fantasies and her desires to make loving sex are natural, but she is challenged to keep in touch with the whole of reality.

We should pay attention to what sexual fantasies tell us about ourselves and about our relationships with people. What kind of person am I in fantasies as contrasted with my everyday self? Am I assertive and adventurous in sexual fantasies and docile and timid in everyday life? How do I act in fantasy? Sexual fantasies can help us discover our limits. Through them we can learn about ourselves to promote growth rather than immaturity or fixation.

To do this we must claim, name, and explain all our sexual feelings. However, this is not an invitation to cultivate and promote genital feelings and fantasies. Rather, honest and truthful acceptance of spontaneous feelings and fantasies can help us to understand what is happening. Genital feelings give more than a physical message; fantasies reveal more than mere genitality. Respect should enable us to be open to the various meanings revealed in genitality. Because sex is an articulation of the whole person, it can be an opportunity to learn from and about oneself.

This woman has a healthy attitude toward fantasies: "I try to learn about myself from my fantasies. Sometimes, my fantasies are too physical. This tells me that I am capable of being less than I want to be. I try to bring love into sex. Usually, I imagine being in an affectionate relationship where the man is very thoughtful and gentle. And I am not only a recipient of this affection; I respond in kind. Genital sex may not even occur. When it does, it is part of the whole experience. Such fantasies tell me what I really want—a respectful and gentle love, a true sharing. Though mere physical sex can be exciting, it leaves me empty. I have learned that it's not what is best for me, nor what I really need and want."

Positive amplification

Positive amplification is helpful in promoting respect and integration. Instead of repressing, escaping, or gratifying genital feelings, amplification involves extending, deepening, and enriching fantasies, dreams, and reality. It does not countenance willful activation or encouragement of genital feelings; it demands respect for genital impulses as parts of one's whole self. Negative amplification, however, could involve stimulation or promotion of genital desires for immediate satisfaction.

To look for the spiritual within the genital is helpful for maintaining a wholistic perspective. For example, "an erect penis" in itself is not an experiential reality; only a man who has an erect penis is real. Likewise, there is no such independent reality as an "erect clitoris"; only a woman who has an erect clitoris. To respect these physical realities leads to integration, wholeness. The physical changes in genitalia can indicate that the whole person is standing out, moving toward, yearning for, and is receptive of intimacy with another. They can express the fact that one's whole being—not just the genital being—is seeking intimacy and interpersonal fulfillment. Genital yearning is a distinct way of uncovering the transcendent dynamic of being human: desire for union with another.

Of course, one can refuse the call to integration and focus exclusively on the physical dimension of genitality. However, surrender to the desire for immediate pleasure impedes growth in wholeness and therefore happiness. Failure to respect and promote wholeness frustrates spiritual growth.

Too many of us neither believe in ourselves nor trust our spiritual selves; consequently, we dissociate rather than integrate our genital sexuality. Even though we abstain from extramarital sex, we may separate spirituality and sexuality in our marriage. Instead of fostering the unity of love and sex, we maintain a dualism between the two or focus exclusively on genitality. Marital sex can be just as physicalistic and spiritless as nonmarital recreational sex. Moreover, it probably has more negative consequences within marriage than outside of it.

Healthy amplification employs creative control. Instead of habitually satisfying, repressing, or blindly restricting fantasies and feelings, the individual uses discipline to follow the truth of his or her genitality. This control is not violent; it does not treat the genital self as an enemy. Rather, it involves "being with"; that is, approaching the genital self as a friend. The relaxed discipline and attentive freedom in creative control enables a person to test limits, expand horizons, and deepen values.

Sometimes genital feelings are so strong and loud that they

"silence" the messages of other feelings. For instance, a man may so intensely yearn to be genitally intimate with a woman that he forgets the other kinds of intimacy and loses creative control of himself. He treats himself and the woman as merely genital beings. Creative listening would help him to hear more than genital feelings.

Tucked within the clamor and confusion of genital feelings is the drive to become whole with another. Are we able to listen for the whisper of spiritual longings within our genitality?

"I hear what you're saying," one man confessed, "but when I get horny it's really difficult to appreciate the whole person. I think you're right about responding to the whole person, but it's as if my genital desires take over. I guess that's when I have to get some distance. In a sense, I have to sober up. I have to make a strong effort to remind myself that the woman is not a sex object for my pleasure. She has feelings and values just like my sister or mother. I have to see that she is just as human as they are."

Instead of concentrating on only a part of a person, we can be open to another's integrity (wholeness) and experience his or her dignity (worth) as well as our own. This creative seeing involves cutting through the surface (transcendence) to regard and appreciate sex as a revelation of the whole person and as a yearning for communion. To interpret genital yearnings as biological drives alone, or as lustful needs, is a one-sided perception. It is also a violation of the dignity of human personhood, of our spiritual or communal dimension.

Imagine a man sexually attracted to a girl who finds himself admiring her physical appearance. Instead of identifying her with her bodiliness and thinking of how "to make out" or "to make her," he can amplify his perception and thereby appreciate her, even though he may never speak to her. For instance, he may look at the way she presents herself—the way she dresses and expresses herself—and wonder what she intends to say to herself and others. What does her body language communicate? Is she stiff or relaxed, aloof or friendly, sad or glad, scared or confident? It is important that he see her as a member of the same human community as he. Such creative reflection can help the man become intimate with her even though she remains a stranger. Instead of taking a one-sided look, he regards her more wholly and realistically.

Again, imagine a woman who fantasizes about making love with a man. Instead of blocking her feelings prematurely, she amplifies her fantasies to see where they will lead her. Instead of stopping her fantasy short at petting, genital play, or orgasm, she might consider what is likely to happen after sex. Do he and she suddenly disappear? Is everything over and forgotten? Is there a future? If so, what kind? What real difference does such intimacy make? Will it make her more mature? better? healthier? more loving? more committed? What are the real consequences likely to be? Such healthy amplification involves an extension of the possible consequences of fantasy and links the fantasy with reality. It makes fantasy more real.

Humor

Humor, according to empirical and clinical research, can help us listen, see, and control. Humor brings life into perspective. Zest and hilarity affirm our true place in life. Humor is the springboard to the divine. Moreover, humor heals; it activates processes that promote health. Humor makes us laugh, settle down, and heal. Humor invites us to dance with life and to sing a song of joy. Without humor, we rob ourselves. Humor is the gateway to saving grace.

Prayer

Prayer is the most directly spiritual way to cope with and integrate sexuality. Indeed, spirituality is the paramount dynamic of integration; prayer is the primary way to maintain, nourish, and facilitate spiritual growth. To pray when pressured to engage in or while involved in sex fosters integration, engenders a wholistic perspective, and gives power.

Some people consider prayer a foolish endeavor—an illusion. Indeed, this can be so. Authentic prayer, however, is a realistic and practical way to help one become his or her sexual self. Even from a clinical perspective, prayer is crucial to the sexual health and wholeness of single vowed celibates and married persons.

Prayer is the best way to connect with God, our higher power. At anytime, but especially when we feel powerless and unable to manage, prayer is therapeutic. Through it we give our life and will to God, evoking a power beyond our individual selves. God gives us strength to face both the darkness and the light in ourselves, to be open to community, to maintain and promote our spiritual life. Prayer is not pie in the sky fantasy; it is an effective approach supported by empirical and clinical research.

Through prayer we realize that we are more than individuals, that we are in communion with others and with God. We affirm that our sustaining source of healthy and happy living is brotherhood and sisterhood in, with, and through God. Prayer encourages us to broaden our perspective and to allow the spiritual to have impact on us. To work with a power that is greater than ourselves, to live with a Transcendent Presence that helps and heals is essential to wholistic sexuality.

Besides explicitly sacred practices such as liturgical worship, meditation, and personal and group prayer, an orientation of love is vital. To live a life of love helps us to admit our dependence on the Divine and to keep a wholistic perspective. Lived prayer and contemplative presence pressure us to see and respond to sexuality in healthy ways.

Prayer contains the possibility of miracles. More likely, however, God grants us help to achieve the serenity that enables us to accept, understand, and cope with the challenges, frustrations, and opportunities of sexuality. Those who do not pray rob themselves of the most effective source for becoming healthy (sexual) persons. It is foolish not to pray; prayer is our reason for being.

CHAPTER 8

Nonhealthy
Genital Behavior

In an earlier chapter, I proposed that marriage is the only situation that affords the proper time, place, and commitment for healthy and good genital sex. Although the state of marriage does not guarantee healthy genital sex, other situations do not offer this opportunity.

Also, I suggested that genital sex calls for love. Genital love is a sacred and sensual experience; it demands wholeness and holiness if it is to bear fruit in healthy and spiritual living. Love is the decision to promote the best possible health for self and other. In genital love, one experiences the union of spirituality and sexuality. Genital sex is beautiful when those who share it are affirmed, appreciated, and enjoyed as whole persons. Nevertheless, genital sex can fall short of this intention. In this chapter we will consider forms of nonhealthy genital sex.

Premarital and extramarital sex

Nonmarital sex can be attractive and seductive, especially to those who feel empty and lonely. Such persons are particularly vulnerable to involvement in a genital relationship since sex can numb pain and give the illusion of fulfillment. Emptiness quickly returns, however, often more intensively.

Here are one woman's reflections on this situation: "Sometimes almost anybody would seem better than nobody. When I feel so lonely, I wish someone would hold and hug me. I yearn to be touched, to know I am worthy of being loved. Genital sex isn't really what I'm after, but I know it usually comes with the affection. And the sexual relationship is somehow meaningful—it kind of brings excitement and intimacy to my boring and lonely life. Yet, it doesn't work out; it doesn't really give me what I want and need. Something very important is missing."

There are many kinds of nonmarital sex. For example, recreational genital sex between strangers differs considerably from sex between a couple engaged to be married. In the former situation, the partners are likely using each other for pleasure. Committed lovers do not usually play such games. Although in love, they try to abstain from genital sex because they do not have the proper time and place to experience genital sex in the best way.

Nevertheless, it is difficult when a man and woman genuinely love each other and begin to move sincerely toward genital love. For example, intimate friends, having honest and good intentions, may desire to express their love through sexual intercourse. They seek sexual love and not mere self-satisfaction. But if they engage in genital sex, such lovers find that the activity eventually impedes their growth in love. Such love makes sense in many respects: genital sex can express love while it lessens tension and even increases self-worth. Moreover, abstinence is hard because the goodness of the experience and of the persons involved is evident. In time, however, usually sooner than later, love dissipates. Although the partners probably and understandably dislike saying no, they realize their friendship is being hurt. Extramarital sex impedes and can destroy a friendship. Authentic genital sexuality calls for marital time, place, and commitment.

Some will argue that two unmarried persons living together do have the time, place, and perhaps commitment (temporary) to have healthy sex. This kind of relationship is meaningful, but not in the same way as the friends' or engaged couple's relationship; it lacks the permanent and faithful commitment that genital behavior needs. Although the situation is more convenient than that of persons not living together, proper commitment is lacking. Casual or sincere living together is popular today. It is not recommended, however; it falls short of healthy living. This is evident in the following remarks of someone in a "living together" situation: "I really care for Jim and I think he really cares for me. Besides, sharing the same apartment saves on rent and food bills. We get along pretty good, too. But I wonder if we will ever get married, or if I even want to. We seldom talk about it. What really makes me uneasy is that I know he can walk out at any time. For that matter, so can I. I feel like I'm always walking on eggshells, like I have to be too good. It's as if there isn't room for argument or even disagreements. I always have to be at my best. It's like playing house."

Contrary to popular opinion, studies indicate that living together does not increase the likelihood of a good marriage. In fact, people who live together are less likely to succeed in marriage. It seems that the lack of a commitment, affirmed legally and sacramentally, weakens the relationship. The experience does not give assurance of permanence to a potential marriage; the opposite is more likely.

Recreational sex (premarital or extramarital sex for mere pleasure) can make sense also. It satisfies genital needs and gives pleasure. Since any sexual activity involves some spiritual aspect, there is also union—the spiritual is hidden and violated, but it is present nevertheless. The yearning for union (the spiritual dimension) is the primary but hidden reason for any sexual activity, even recreational sex. But what the person unconsciously wants and needs—healthy communion—is not realized. Again, when we do not treat one another as whole persons, we block and violate the spiritual dynamic of unity. Consequently, we feel empty, incomplete, unwhole. Although we may experience fleeting moments of being one with another, it quickly disappears and fails to foster growth in the other sectors of our lives. This momentary and counterfeit peace causes progressive alienation and loneliness. To separate sex (body) and love (spirit) is to fragment ourselves. Although we may honestly and mutually agree to recreational sex, we nevertheless exploit and violate each other.

Subtle, sad sex can occur in marriage, too. Partners who consistently engage in "quickie sex" to satisfy genital needs do not have good or healthy sex. A typical example of this is the husband who has a quick orgasm, using his wife as a sperm receptacle, and then falls asleep without regard for his wife. The woman experiences little enjoyment, feeling used and abused. Moreover, a woman can be just as exploitive and selfish. This practice leads to alienation rather than unity.

Excepting marriage, all forms of loving should exclude genital relations. Free from marital limits and responsibilities, single and/or celibate lovers have the opportunity to perfect all modes of intimacy except the genital and those that foster or lead to it. Unlike the married, single persons do not focus their love on one human being. This does not mean they cannot be intimate with another person; such intimacy simply does not take a marital form.

Masturbation

Masturbation is a common form of genital gratification. By age twenty-one, most men have masturbated. Women masturbate less; however, the percentage gap between male and female masturbation is narrowing. Increasingly more people feel little or no compunction about masturbating. This was not always the case.

Different Views

In the "old days" (not very long ago), many people were taught that masturbation is one of the worst sins. It was suggested that masturbation was a cause of mental and physical illness, even that surgical intervention could be a treatment for masturbation. It seems masturbation evoked more guilt than dishonesty or injustice. In those days it was common to overemphasize sexual sins. Masturbation—even the mere thought of it—guaranteed a one-way ticket to hell. Sexuality was treated as an "enemy" or as exclusively a means for procreation rather than a gift and opportunity from God for spiritual and psychological growth.

Because of the negative assessment of sexuality, the approach to sexual feelings was to ignore or repress them. As we have seen, however, denial increases tension rather than purges it, resulting in frustration, anxiety, and guilt. Individuals, acting sincerely, tried to silence the potentially redemptive message of their uncomfortable feelings. Consequently, they escaped self-confrontation by overindulgence (eating, drinking, working), irritable behavior (toward authorities, peers, or subjects), or acting out (with others and/or self in fantasy and/or reality). When masturbation (acting out) was the coping mechanism for repressed or nonintegrated sexuality, a circular and frustrating pattern would emerge: masturbation to relieve tension, followed by guilt, followed by tension, which led again to masturbation and so on and on.

The "new ways" are expression and guiltlessness. Many health specialists consider masturbation a sensible source of pleasure, a convenient tension reducer, a productive way to realize body awareness and potential—in general, a healthy practice. Satisfying "my own" needs, insisting that "my body is mine," and having "good" feelings are conventional justifications. Since discomfort is assumed to indicate something wrong, the practices of suppression, mortification, and sublimation are judged masochistic, old-fashioned, or simply naive and dumb.

From a wholistic perspective, I personally support neither the new nor the old position. I contend that masturbation is seldom unhealthy in and of itself. Unlike many professionals, however, I do not believe masturbation should be recommended. Psychologically, masturbation is neither a one-way ticket to hell nor to heaven. Masturbation is an earthly matter, neither unhealthy nor healthy. It is a conventional way of reducing tension, evoking pleasure, and acquiring a degree of normal maintenance.

Sociologically, masturbation is "normal" in that most people at some time in their lives practice it more or less. It falls within the parameters of "normal" and often expected behavior. Psychologically, masturbation can be considered "normal" because it can temporarily reduce tension that may make life easier immediately (though not better) and help one to cope in the short run. Nevertheless, although masturbation can be considered "normal" in this sense, I contend it is not healthy because it impedes spiritual growth.

The context

To understand the dynamics of masturbation, it is important to look at the life of one who masturbates. The act should be seen in light of a total process. One element of this context is age. For example, adolescents usually feel more strongly than children and adults the urgency and confusion of new genital desires. Also, they experience peer and cultural pressure to satisfy them. An adult who has repressed his or her genital feelings may masturbate for reasons like those of an adolescent: urgency, novelty, pleasure, curiosity, environmental pressure.

Frequency and intensity are also important factors. Masturbating once a month differs from doing it once a day in terms of psychosocial and spiritual impact. Compulsive masturbation involves a significant part of one's life. In contrast, some people generally abstain from masturbation but periodically "act out" for a relatively short time. Others follow a cyclic pattern: they allow tension to build up, periodically relieve it, then wait for it to increase again.

Here's one adolescent's reflection on masturbation: "I'm not real guilty about it, but I'm not proud of it either. Most of the guys do it at some time or another. There are some guys who don't masturbate, so I guess it can be done. I masturbate when I'm especially horny, or when I'm bored and have a lot of time. It relieves the tension, but I have to admit that the tension always returns. Masturbating doesn't seem to get you anywhere."

Intensity of involvement is significant also. The amount of time as well as quantity and quality of self-investment determine the impact masturbation has on one's life. Someone who masturbates daily for an hour with intense fantasy as the primary source of intimacy will differ significantly from a person who masturbates infrequently and has healthy experiences of intimacy.

Seductiveness

Masturbation is particularly seductive because it is an easy and accessible way to reduce tension and to explore genital feelings and fantasies without interpersonal vulnerability, responsibility, and accountability. It seems we have a license to masturbate almost whenever we feel like it. We need not worry about other people or social consequences; it can be kept to oneself.

Part of masturbation's lure is the safe secrecy of fantasy: one does not have to risk rejection, embarrassment, or failure. It gives the illusion of being invulnerable, open, and perfect. Instead of engaging in mature relationships, the individual can create a world of make-believe people where anything is possible and there are no limits.

A subtle attraction of masturbation is that the initial choice often emerges from nongenital experiences: boredom, anxiety, and especially loneliness may pressure us to masturbate. Masturbation can numb the discomfort of emptiness and incompleteness and promise some semblance of being one with self and other. But these rewards are short-lived. The frustrating irony is that the escape from loneliness actually impedes the attainment of the true goal: intimacy.

The hidden sense and nonsense

Masturbation involves a yearning for intimacy and completeness. We have seen that this transcendent dynamic is evident even in the physiological changes of sexual excitement: the body visibly moves out for more than oneself. Fantasy, also, manifests a desire to be intimate with another and/or to go beyond oneself. This transcendent dynamic can be considered a manifestation of the spiritual in genital arousal. The hidden meaning is that we are being moved to go beyond ourselves to another, to more than mere self-containment.

The folly of masturbation (as well as recreational sex) is that it silences the urge to love. The individual aborts an opportunity for growth and ends up being more empty and more lonely. Though masturbation can numb the yearning for intimacy, its satisfaction is momentary and not growth-oriented. Masturbation turns oneself inward, making one intimate with self while impeding one's true longing: authentic intimacy with another.

A particular danger of frequent masturbation is narcissism: pleasurable self-preoccupation. Someone who masturbates habitually is inclined toward immediate gratification and to seeing others in terms of self-satisfaction. A married person who masturbates or who has masturbated frequently and intensely in the past may unconsciously use his or her spouse for self-satisfaction. Even though this selfish motive may be unconscious, it nevertheless hurts intimacy.

Masturbation is superficial also, maximizing the physical and minimizing the spiritual. Sexual gratification without involvement of the spiritual self is only surface contact that leads to shallow living. Engaging in nonintegrated sex eventually leads to greater frustration; what we seek—integral and ongoing growth—eludes us.

Here are the comments of a man who recognizes his folly: "Masturbation is a habit with me and I wish I could stop it. I know I go off into fantasy too much and read too many pornographic books. Actually, I'm ashamed to admit that I'm scared of real involvement. I guess I use masturbation as a substitute for real intimacy. But it's no fun being lonely. Maybe someday I'll stop and go for the real thing."

Helping self and others

When trying to help ourselves or others, we should distinguish between therapeutic help and normative evaluation. Maturity consists of bearing the tension between what is and what should be. Normatively, masturbation should neither be condoned nor recommended. To preserve and promote norms, I offer my viewpoints in teaching, writing, and conversation. As a person responsible to and sometimes for others, I am obliged to give my view. I believe, for instance, that to encourage someone to masturbate or engage in any form of nonmarital genital behavior is to cheat that person. We also cheat others when we do not give a point of view. A viewpoint is essential to dialogue and growth.

On the other hand, a therapeutic approach suspends normative evaluation in order to explore sense and nonsense. When I am asked or when I think it my responsibility, I give my standards; otherwise, I accept (neither condoning nor condemning) masturbation or nonmarital sex and encourage the person to enter the process of self-exploration through self-disclosure. Although we should not sanction nonmarital gratification for self or for others, we can accept such behavior, without condemning or recommending it, in the search for wholistic growth.

It is difficult to help oneself and others; our educational programs for coping with and integrating sexual desires are often very deficient. Many of us are left with two options: to repress or to satisfy. Such a choice offers very little freedom. We are told to "integrate" our sexuality, but few helpful suggestions are given for doing it.

To help ourself and others, it is important to look behind the mask of masturbation and see what is hidden and neglected. Masturbation, like genital intercourse, is often a sign of more basic issues. Usually, some part of our lives (activity, thinking, feeling) is being overemphasized, sexuality is not being integrated, or feelings (loneliness, boredom, frustration) are being avoided. Masturbatory acts tell something about our whole lives.

To move closer to the ideal of integration, the following suggestions may be helpful. It is foolish to underestimate the force of habit. Our body can be conditioned to yearn for tranquilizing but negative experiences. Realize that masturbation gives immediate rewards that reinforce the habit and increase the likelihood of its occurrence. The individual who masturbates compulsively, for example, is caught in a discouraging circle: the more he masturbates, the more difficult it is to control. Good intentions and willpower are not enough; in a sense, our body has a will of its own. Suppression, anticipation, sublimation, and integration of sexual desires, as well as humor and prayer, are significant in reducing the strength of habit.

Consider this wise approach: "When I'm tempted to masturbate, I try to get busy or involved with others. When this is not possible, I try to keep God in the picture. Sure, I pray, but that's not all that I mean. I try to see God's spirit in the person I'm fantasizing about, and I try to see my God in me. When I let God stay in the picture, my experience is different. And when I forget about God, I get in bad shape or have little power to resist. Then I am inclined to see myself and the other mainly as sexual bodies without the spirit. Afterward, I feel spiritless."

It also helps to chart recurring patterns of masturbation. We may discover regular times and places when and where masturbation is likely to occur, or feelings and moods that precede masturbation. Anticipating that we are more vulnerable at certain times, in certain places, and in certain moods can help us to monitor and take care of ourselves. We can take measures to safeguard our vulnerable self.

This man's comment is insightful: "I know I'm especially vulnerable at night and on weekends. I'm especially careful at those times to be busy or not to be preoccupied with the possibility of masturbating. It seems that when I am bored, lonely, or generally uptight, I am more prone to masturbate. Not that masturbation is all that bad, but it's nothing to brag about either. Besides, it's a waste of time and really doesn't help except to relieve some tension—but only for awhile. So, I'm careful at certain times. Masturbation is something I choose not to do."

We should also discern and discuss the kind(s) of guilt we have. We should experience more than "superego" guilt, the kind that comes from breaking a rule and, in the extremes, creates feelings of damnation. Some superego guilt is needed at times, but when it is the only kind of guilt, we are not mature. It is always tempting to act as children who follow the letter of the law, or as adolescents who judge reality only in terms of absolute ideals—good or bad, meaningful or meaningless.

It is better to cultivate a mature sense of guilt. One should feel guilty for masturbating not primarily because a rule has been broken or because one is revealed as less than perfect. Rather, the guilt should stem from the failure to become what one realistically can become. Mature guilt calls us to appreciate the good and to seek a better life, not to focus primarily on the negative or what we did wrong.

Good books on sexuality should be read and discussed. Knowing the so-called facts and possibilities, both pro and con, helps. Many books on sexuality, however, have questionable values and some are simply immoral. Authors who recommend masturbation as a healthy practice, for example, do not take a wholistic approach; usually they exclude the spiritual dimension.

Books are usually better than movies. Movies (often under the guise of sex education) pressure us to move at their pace, whereas books give us more leeway to assimilate at our own pace. Moreover, graphic illustrations in movies are often ageist, sexist, and racist. Rarely do movies depict old couples. Also, they are often sexist in that they follow a male model of sexuality.

Graphics can play havoc on unconscious desires and fantasies. When we watch and discuss movies that portray sexual intercourse, masturbation, and other forms of erotic behavior, we can give ourselves and others a false impression of openness and security. Intellectually we seem fine, but our unconscious and affective lives may present a different story. After the aura of openness is over, images and desires engendered by genital graphics emerge in dreams, fantasies, and interpersonal relations. With good intentions, we hinder rather than help our sexual lives.

To view masturbation as a challenge to growth, the individual must listen to and learn from the uncomfortable feelings that underlie and motivate masturbation. Feelings of disembodiment, fatigue, loneliness, boredom, and depression tell something about one's life. Instead of silencing the message through masturbation, we should listen to their invitations to grow holy as well as wholly. We should strive to see the Spirit hidden behind the mask of masturbation. Instead of remaining only within ourselves, we should listen to the call of transcendence, the call to go beyond ourselves.

Homosexuality

Homosexuality has become a controversial as well as a debated and unsettling issue. Some people think homosexuality is a perversion, a disease, not good at best. Others contend that homosexuals, while maintaining a different sexual preference, can function as well as heterosexuals. Many are not sure and wonder about homosexuality.

Homosexuality is the condition of experiencing in oneself an erotic preference for members of one's own sex. Someone who frequently yearns to fantasize and act out genital relations exclusively with one's own sex may be homosexual, though not necessarily so. It is important to realize that people do not choose their sexual orientation. Homosexuals do not initially choose to be "gay"; rather, they find themselves oriented in this way just as heterosexuals discover they are "straight."

Homosexuals are persons who feel comfortable and affirmed when intimate with the same sex; with the other sex they may feel weak, resentful, scared, or simply indifferent or less comfortable when genital intimacy is possible or occurs. However, most homosexual men are comfortable with women in situations where genital intimacy is unlikely or impossible. They often demonstrate greater sensitivity toward women than heterosexual men. And since women do not have to worry about genital involvement, many women are more comfortable with homosexual men.

Theories about homosexuality

Studies of homosexuality are not conclusive, though there are many theories. Some scientists assert that homosexuality has a hereditary and genetic basis. Others propose an imbalance of sex hormones. Still others conjecture that during a critical period in childhood a preferred sexual object or person can become firmly entrenched in the mind.

A popular theory is that homosexuality is caused by certain psychosocial pressures and conditioning factors in a person's environment. One study revealed that eighty-four percent of male homosexuals, as opposed to eighteen percent of male heterosexuals, felt that their father had been emotionally distant and indifferent. This theory suggests that a homosexual is seeking a caring and affirmative man. Nevertheless, this does not mean that all boys who lack a caring father will be homosexual or that all homosexuals had a distant father.

Theories of female homosexuality are even less developed and valid. The most widespread hypothesis, far from conclusive, proposes that homosexual women come from dysfunctional families consisting of a cruel father and a martyred mother. The theory adds that lesbians frequently have traits related to dominance, status seeking, intellectual efficiency, and endurance. These traits compensate for the possibility that a male will cause once more the chaos he did when the woman was a child.

Research shows interesting differences between male and female homosexuals. For instance, a lesbian is more likely to have longer periods of attachment to one partner. Male relationships, on the other hand, are usually short-lived and throughout a life span include many partners. Furthermore, the occurrence of exclusive and partial homosexuality among women is two-thirds of that found among men. Also, two-thirds of declared lesbians are bisexual; that is, they have had and/or will have heterosexual experience.

It is important to recognize the non-homogenital motivations in the lives of homosexuals. For instance, some homosexuals feel compelled to visit homosexual places by a sense of adventure that brings excitement and risk. Some seek out other homosexuals in order to "be with"—to find acceptance as a member of a community and to escape the alienation of being labeled "one of them." Some homosexuals, especially when bored and lonely, desire a setting where they can be themselves without pretense. Still others, living a highly cognitive and disembodied life, periodically crave excitement.

Many homosexuals come to feel as if they live in two worlds: the so-called "straight" world and the "gay" world. In time, this dual life not only becomes psychologically and spiritually distressing, but also physically exhausting. It is simply very difficult in terms of time and energy to be involved in two worlds. Finding time and space for homosexual involvement becomes a tedious and weary task. Stress sometimes pressures a person to choose one of the two life-styles.

We must be careful not to categorize homosexuals. All homosexuals are not the same. Actually, it is better to speak of "homosexualities" than of "homosexuality." To identify persons with a part of them—in this case their sexuality—is unjust and harmful. Homosexuals, after all, differ as much as heterosexuals. For instance, most homosexuals are not effeminate; effeminate men are not necessarily homosexual. All hairdressers are not gay; all athletes are not straight. Some homosexuals are unhealthy and need help; others are normal in that they cope, succeed, and look and act as most other people. Still others are healthy.

It is my view that homosexuality (understood as homogenitality) is not healthy, but that homosexual persons can be healthy. Homogenital behavior is not healthy because the transcendent dimension of genital love is aborted. Unlike heterogenital relations, homogenital relations neither go beyond themselves nor can they be procreative—a sacred sign of transcendence. What many homosexuals are seeking—to feel permanently at home and to grow perpetually in love—does not progressively and faithfully occur in homogenital relations.

Opponents of this view argue that homosexual marriages do exist. In fact, little data exists to support the existence of such permanent relationships. The genital relations of those few who do live together for a long time are usually absent or minimal so that the ongoing commitment is more aptly described as a celibate friendship than a marriage. Or, a homosexual couple may live together with functional commitment but without the fidelity that genital relations call for. That is, they are more or less promiscuous. As in heterosexual marriages, this unfaithfulness cannot be condoned.

Some people contend that homosexuality can be healthy when it fosters growth. These people make a distinction between promiscuous homosexuality which is considered not healthy, and homosexuality accompanied by care and fidelity, which is considered healthy. As I indicated above, research suggests that long-term homosexual marriages exist (though rarely); however, such relationships lack fidelity. My view is that genital experiences between persons of the same gender do not foster ongoing wholistic growth.

In short, homogenital relationships run contrary to the process of authentic genitality; that is, homogenital intimacy does not promote the progressive and transcendent growth that is possible in marital heterogenital relationships. Of course, all heterogenital relationships do not promote integral and ongoing growth. However, such growth is possible. Many homosexuals are healthy, but homogenital intimacy is incongruent with the wholistic model.

Some persons, controlling their homosexual cravings, become celibate homosexuals. Although their orientation is primarily homosexual, they love and function well with both sexes. Although they may have homosexual feelings and fantasies, they never or rarely engage in homogenital relations. This is painfully difficult at times, but their sexual desires challenge and motivate them to grow in chaste celibacy.

This can seem and may be unfair, particularly to a homosexual person. Homosexuals are challenged, as many unmarried heterosexuals are, to control and integrate their genital desires without gratifying them. Certainly this can be difficult. Furthermore, a homosexual does not have the option to marry a person whom he prefers, whereas a heterosexual does. In this sense homosexuality is unfair, but ideally it can be accepted as a challenge to growth.

Consider the feelings of this thirty-five-year-old man: "In adolescence I noticed that I was different than most others. I simply did not care to be intimate with girls, but I did desire it with guys. This confused and scared me. It was a heavy and lonely burden to carry. And I felt sad and angry when my friends would joke about gays—queers and faggots as they called them. Although I've had some homosexual experiences since then, I've usually kept myself in control. Sometimes it's extremely difficult. It seems unfair. I did not choose to be gay, but that's what I am and I accept it. I know I'm not sick because I'm gay. I'm just as healthy as anyone else."

Pseudo-homosexualities

Constitutional homosexuality differs from transitory, situational, or pseudo-homosexualities—homogenital relationships that are relatively short-term. For example, persons who have had homogenital experiences perhaps once or several times in their life, or who have had a so-called affair, are probably not homosexual. A few homogenital experiences do not necessarily constitute a homogenital life-style or orientation.

Here are the comments of a man who expresses unfortunate and unnecessary confusion and guilt: "I've felt uneasy and guilty about something that happened sixteen years ago. My friend and I got sexually involved over a period of seven months. We got very close and shared a lot. I've never been so close to anyone. Sometimes we got physical with each other, did some hugging and kissing, and on a couple of occasions some mutual masturbation. It drove me nuts to think I might be gay. It was a heavy and secret burden I had to carry within me. I was scared to talk to anyone about it. I'm glad I talked about it. Now, I don't feel so weird or alien anymore."

This man is not homosexual. He had some homogenital experiences, probably because his intimacy evoked repressed sexuality that surfaced too quickly to control and integrate. This man also had desires for and fantasies about women, a symptom of being heterosexual, but he diagnosed himself falsely. Such pseudo-homosexuality is not rare, especially when a heterosexual relationship is difficult to attain.

Transitory or situational homosexuality occurs particularly between friends who are very sensitive but who have learned to repress or to rigidly restrict their feelings. For example, Don comes from a good but puritanical family and has learned to restrict affective expression. One day he finds himself involved with Mike, a friend who comfortably expresses affectivity. The men care for each other and become so emotionally and intimately involved that they fall into genital behavior as a mode of expressing their love. Instead of identifying themselves as homosexuals, Don and Mike should stop and learn from their relationship. Outsiders should refrain from calling them impure, evil, or queer, and evaluate their relationship in light of solid psychological and spiritual principles—and with compassion. The two men should get help from a competent professional who understands and appreciates the sense and nonsense of homosocial love, affection, and intimacy.

Consider, too, the case of Joan and Lisa. They never or seldom had experienced a trusting and affirmative relationship before they became close friends. In the initial phases of their friendship they feel that everything is possible and nothing impossible: they want to be intimate in every way, including the genital, and though they experience some guilt, they are also ecstatic. Both women, because of their infatuation, feel more alive than ever before. But their heavenly state will end sooner or later. After divinizing each other, they will probably experience a "negative stage" when they will begin to focus on each other's limits and imperfections. Consequently, they will be more vulnerable to hurt, bitterness, resentment, and jealousy. If they are willing, however, they can develop an integral friendship that incorporates both their divine and demonic dimensions.

If Joan and Lisa can come to realize that their genital experiences do not nurture their friendship, they can learn to set limits on their expressions of affection and abstain from genital love. These women are not lesbians; they are loving women who originally repressed themselves affectively, then became too physically involved. Although their homogenital experiences should not be condoned, neither should the women be condemned to a life of guilt and alienation or be diagnosed as homosexuals.

Every deep friendship is special and intimate. Friends see each other unlike anyone else sees them; they have and are something special. Moreover, the best of friendships are exclusive: they do exclude others in some way. For instance, friends understand each other in ways that no one else can understand them. Exclusivity in friendship, however, should eventually help the friends become more inclusive—more sensitive and compassionate with others. Friendship should liberate rather than shackle us. Genital behavior between friends is not healthy for either heterosexuals or homosexuals; it eventually destroys the friendship. Although a friendship can be very intimate, it does not include the kind of commitment, time, and space needed for wholistic genital love.

Homosocial intimacy—the way a person relates to the same sex socially and affectively—is a problem that is often more threatening to men than to women. This is partly because our culture makes it difficult for men to be close with one another. If one is male, anything more than a handshake is ridiculed or seen as a perversion. Male affectivity is certainly not fostered.

Another form of homosocial intimacy is "chumminess," an indirect way of expressing affection. Frequent gestures or words of affection and semi-erotic kidding are unlikely to betray latent homosexuality; they more likely indicate a clumsy or less than mature sexuality. However, this homosocial sexual behavior can be okay in moderation when it offers a safe and fun way to express and learn about affection.

Personally and culturally, women are usually more comfortable in the homosocial realm. They have learned to be more adept interpersonally and their self-esteem often is linked with care. Paradoxically, women may feel personally freer—even pressured—to express affection with one another than men are. Women who are not close to anyone may feel more frustrated and lonely than men. These feelings can lead a person to unnecessary guilt or to premature or immature intimacy—or it can motivate to develop mature relations with people.

Responding to homosexuality

To help others we always must begin with ourselves. We should know our own assumptions, feelings, thoughts, and values about homosexuality and homosexuals. The first step is to listen to self: What do I feel and think? Am I genuinely concerned? How and why am I concerned? Self-discernment should free us from mixed feelings and free us for caring effectively.

It is important to differentiate between homosexuals as persons and their homosexual acts. Instead of identifying homosexuals with their sexual acts—something neither just nor helpful—we should seek to understand them in light of their entire lives. A relative or teacher can be a healthy homosexual who never actualizes sexual impulses; it is possible to live a fundamentally good life but have infrequent and transitory sexual experiences. Also it is helpful to ascertain what a homosexual experience means to the involved persons—how and in what circumstances did it occur? As we have seen, friends who have known emotional restrictions differ significantly from committed homosexuals. It is not my intention here to condone or support homosexual acts; rather, the purpose is to foster understanding, compassion, growth, and community—brotherhood and sisterhood.

Another guideline in understanding homosexual activities is to determine if heterophobia—fear of heterosexual involvement—is present. By focusing on the same sex, some people seek to escape their fear of the opposite sex. A man who focuses exclusively on men may be escaping his fear of women. When confronted with women, such a man may become withdrawn, condescending, or just plain scared. Consequently, he may be vulnerable to homosexual intimacy as a way of gratifying sexual desires. A woman, too, may desire intimacy with a woman because she never learned to be intimate with men. Perhaps her past experiences were traumatic—she was abused or rejected by men, particularly her father and brothers. Her quasi-homosexual experiences are likely to be a cover for other problems.

Some people seek sexual satisfaction with the same sex when the other sex is unavailable. This is a tendency in places where only one sex is present. Since such persons usually return to heterosexual involvement, their orientation is basically heterosexual. Whatever the case, the individuals can change their quasi-homosexuality by becoming more aware of and working through their heterosexual conflict or immature sexuality.

A fundamental step is to manifest in ourselves what we want to see in others. Do you and I manifest healthy sexuality and love in our everyday behavior? Do we recognize and behave according to the principle that homosexuals, pseudo-homosexuals, and quasi-homosexuals are radically the same as us—persons? Instead of calling homosexuals "them," can we embrace homosexuals as brothers and sisters of the same human family? The most important response is to show and share a life of love. Without this basic, preverbal presence, other forms of help are ineffective and possibly harmful.

How to help ourselves

What can you do if someone, particularly a friend, pressures you to enter a homosexual relationship? First, it is good to take stock of oneself. What part might you have in the relationship? Do your expressions of affection unintentionally elicit different feelings in your friend? Are you unconsciously seeking or wondering what it would be like to engage in homosexual love? Are your conscious intentions (thoughts) the same as your unconscious intentions (feelings)? If you are chaste (without selfishness and with love), can you understand the sense and nonsense of homosexuality? Can you foster love for all people, including homosexuals, and thereby foster healthy relationships?

Understanding and acceptance liberate us for coping competently and compassionately. Instead of rejecting a friend or making (him or her) feel guilty or bad, one can say "no" as an affirmation of one's love. More concretely, one can give reasons for refusing homosexuality and for accepting friendship. In this way a friend will feel accepted without having his or her proposal for genital acting out condoned or reinforced. Both parties will gain a deeper appreciation of the friendship.

One man expressed this challenging dilemma in these words: "I was shocked when Sid, my friend, expressed his desire to have sex with me. I had no idea of his homosexual feelings. At first I felt like punching him in the mouth or throwing up. Wow, was I homophobic. Instead, I said no, and we talked about our feelings. We worked it through. He respects me, and though I disagree with gay activity, I respect him. We're still friends."

What can and should we do if we are involved in a homosexual relationship? First of all, we should stop. Stopping calls for discipline, which includes suppression. Another help is to anticipate and sublimate one's sexual feelings and to seek to integrate sexuality and spirituality. The challenge is to appreciate the wholeness of self and others so that chaste love is fostered.

Moreover, we should listen to and evaluate our behavior in light of established norms even as we foster care, compassion, and forgiveness. What kind of homosexual am I? Do I feel strong desires to be sexually intimate with the same sex? Do I fantasize only about the same sex? Have I been involved in homosexual acts, or am I involved in transitory sexuality that includes friendship? How does genital sex function in my life? Is it integrated with my entire life or is it a fragmented function? Do I live in two worlds: a sexual world and a spiritual one? What are the nongenital motivations for my homogenital behavior? Instead of repressing the Spirit within me, do I acknowledge God's presence to me—even in my homosexual feelings and acts?

Even though a person remains in the homosexual condition and has periodic desires, he or she can still be healthy. Rather than losing spirit, one can transcend the condition and integrate one's sexuality with love. We are called to live a chaste life of love. This is not easy; no authentic life is. It may be a painfully difficult challenge that calls for discipline and sacrifice that go beyond the ways of conventional living.

Pornography

Since pornography is a major public and private issue, some reflections on this subject are in order. Pornography refers to graphic media, particularly books and movies, whose primary purpose is to excite us genitally. Indeed, pornography is more available than it was in the past. It is easy to acquire "porno" magazines. Many R-rated movies verge on or are pornographic. Hard-core pornography, which includes the "sexploitation" of children and adolescents, is a billion dollar industry.

Pornography is alluring because it "safely" satisfies one's curiosity and stimulates one's fantasy. It offers an idea of what can happen behind closed doors, allowing genital indulgence without the risk of interpersonal involvement. Consider, for example, pornographic books. They allow the user comfortably to engage and test himself or herself with a book's characters or pictures. Unlike other books, they are easy and pleasurable to read. If the user of these books is immature about sex or has other problems, he or she will find easy relief by drifting off into another world.

However, pornographic books and movies are not healthy; they are usually sexist and ageist, and always nonwholistic. Pornography exaggerates the physical dimension of sexuality and minimizes or excludes the spiritual dimension. It attempts to identify a person with sex and to make sex a panacea. Reading porno books encourages us to see people as willing bodies designed exclusively for physical satisfaction. But no person is simply a sexual being; sex is a part of our being. Pornography pressures people to look superficially at self and others and to use them for selfish satisfaction. How easy it is to fool oneself into thinking that sex can replace genuine love.

A man who read several pornographic books in a short time comments: "I felt highly stimulated and yet exhausted, sort of drained out. Although I had a pleasurable time, I felt empty and shallow afterward. I felt sort of odd, like I was less than I am."

This reaction occurs because porno books stimulate only our surface self; consequently, we feel superficial and emptied. Pornography insults its participants by treating them as less than they are. To indulge in pornography is to violate oneself, to treat self as a sex object. Lacking respect for one's whole self is to diminish personal integrity and dignity. A human being deserves and can do better.

Pedophilia

Another issue of increasing public and private concern is pedophilia, a sexual disorder in which a minor (a child or early adolescent) is the love object. Until recently pedophilia, literally meaning love of children, was a problem that evoked ignorance-based anxiety, unnecessary defenses, and inadequate responses. Even when acting with good intentions, authorities treated the pedophile and victim ineffectively—and too often, harmfully. Today, more open and more helpful approaches—legal and therapeutic—are being pursued.

The personality profile of a pedophile fits no one perfectly; it includes all socioeconomic groups, races, and professions. The pedophile is unlikely to be a weird stranger who lurks in the shadows and comes from the other side of the tracks. In fact, about eighty-five percent of potential incidences involve a child and family who know and trust the pedophile. Since the pedophile is attracted to minors, he usually does well working and re-creating with children or adolescents; he is apt to be in a profession or work which gives him access to activities involving minors. This is not to suggest that most adults who deal with minors are pedophiles, or that all pedophiles have ready access to minors. Nevertheless, many pedophiles are in situations which allow them to spend inordinate time, qualitatively and quantitatively, with minors. Indeed, pedophiles seem to enjoy and get more satisfaction from being with minors than in being with peers and other adults.

Most pedophiles appear to be normal, mild-mannered men; about seventy-five percent of them are heterosexual. The pedophile usually looks and functions as well as most people. In certain instances, such as among priests, pedophiles are predominantly homosexual, i.e., they exclusively desire and get sexually involved with boys. Homosexual pedophiles usually are not homosexually active with peers. Moreover, homosexuals usually do not get involved with minors.

Although pedophiles feel tender toward their victims, they still abuse them. Physical force is rare, but another kind of force is used: seduction with affection and the engendering in victims of guilt, fear, and anxiety about hurting the abuser. The sexual offense usually involves kissing, fondling, and masturbation rather than intercourse or sodomy. Finally, pedophiles are usually ashamed, guilty, and confused about their disordered love and sexuality.

Here are the comments of one pedophile: "I don't know why I get involved with pre-puberty girls. I wish I didn't. It tears me apart to know that I do this and that I have to hide this secret burden. Honestly, I really like and try to help the girls, but something gets into me and I go overboard. Sometimes I'll be fine for months, then that demon which seems always to be lurking in the shadows starts to pressure me. It seems that the more I fight it, the stronger it gets. Sometimes I sort of plan to get sexually involved, and other times it just happens. When it happens, I feel satisfied and complete, yet ashamed and guilty.

"Yea, I use all kinds of ploys to protect myself. Like I'll tell her not to say anything to anyone because they won't believe her, or that both of us will get into big trouble. Or, I say I'm sorry and that it will never happen again. I might tell her that I'll deny it and her parents won't believe her. Usually the girl is confused and guilty, so she never tells anyone. I know I need help, but what would people think? What would happen to my career? I'd be ruined."

Another man abnormally loves young adolescent boys. He comments: "You tell me why I do what I do. I wish I knew. I like being with adolescents and they like being with me. I help them and give them experiences and opportunities they would probably never have. Often I get involved with the boy's family; they trust and like me. Everything seems to go well until I find myself wanting to get more intimate. I try to push those feelings out of my mind. Sometimes I'll succeed—nothing sexual occurs. At other times the kid simply grows up, or maybe outgrows me and drifts away. But sometimes I get sexually involved. It's not that I'm some kind of sexual maniac, but....

"I'm usually attracted sexually to a kid who is well-built, athletic, and sensitive. He may be a sullen or troubled fellow. Anyhow, I'm not lurking in the shadows waiting to pounce on someone. When I do get sexually involved, I almost always have known the boy for some time and we have done many things together. Then something happens; it's as if a mood gets the best of me and I can't stop. Sometimes I feel it coming; at other times it catches me by surprise. The boy is usually surprised and confused, though not always.

"I try to tell him that I really care for him, not to let this get in the way. I know it's wrong, but what can I do? Dear God, help me."

Although little is known about the causes of pedophilia, some research data and insights help our understanding and treatment. It is estimated that sixty-five percent of pedophiles were victims of sexual abuse—and they rarely told anyone as children or adults. Sometimes they have repressed such experiences from their own awareness. Some have high levels of biological abnormalities, or higher blood hormone levels. Although biological factors may be present, this is not always the case. All people with higher blood hormone levels are not pedophiles either. Nevertheless, an individual's biochemistry should be tested. In fact, some treatment programs include the use of Depo-Provero to reduce the sex drive by lowering the production of testosterone.

Treatment should also include accepting and working through any psychological pain, particularly past sexual and psychological abuse and psychosexual fixation. Many pedophiles have stopped growing psychosexually due to traumatic sexual experiences in childhood or adolescence; others have fixated because of a particularly satisfying or dissatisfying time of development. Failing to resolve significant issues, these persons continue to be influenced by and/or to return to their unresolved experiences. Whatever the reason, they futilely try to live out and/or resolve their past.

Probably all treatment models demand that pedophiles have as little involvement as possible with children and/or adolescents, particularly when the pedophile is the only adult present. A pedophile who works with or spends considerable time with minors is like an alcoholic who tends bar or is a wine-taster. Pedophiles must abstain from private and frequent contact with minors.

Like most sex offenders and others having addictive behaviors, pedophiles can control their obsessive and compulsive disorder. If the condition is firmly rooted in years of addiction, most therapists admit the orientation cannot be changed, but it can be controlled. It is too early, in my opinion, to determine whether or not a pedophile can change his orientation. However, I have no doubt it can be controlled. Being a diehard idealist, I believe some pedophiles can change their orientation, particularly if they do not have a long history of offenses and continue healthy peer interactions.

The condition of addiction—obsessions and compulsions focused on a substance (food, drugs, etc.), activity (work, sports, etc.), or person (child, adolescent, et al)—offers an effective model for understanding and treating pedophilia. A program patterned on the principles or Twelve Steps of Alcoholics Anonymous is recommended because it is primarily spiritual, rooted in sound psychological principles, and offers the support of brotherhood and sisterhood. On this basis, the pedophile honestly admits that he is powerless over his pedophilia and that his life has become unmanageable. Then, the pedophile affirms that God or a higher power can restore him to sanity; he gives his life and will over to the care of God. With these commitments as a foundation, he regularly participates in group meetings where he is accepted, understood, supported, and confronted while receiving guidance and encouragement to persevere in the Twelve Step program.

The victims of pedophiles should get help to work through their feelings of rejection, threatened sexual identity, impaired psychosexual development, guilt, anger, and overall confusion. Firm and compassionate advice can help affirm and orient the victim sexually. Unfortunately, the knee-jerk reactions of parents and/or other authorities are often as harmful as the sexual offense. For example, they may ask inappropriate questions, minimize or maximize the offense, fail to deal with the victim's feelings, blame the victim, or simply deny that anything happened. Such harmful responses are caused by feelings of shame, embarrassment, anxiety, fear, ignorance, and incompetence.

Pedophilia is unhealthy; it not only violates wholistic growth but is based on pathological processes. The more the pedophile is obsessed about and acts on his disorder, the more unhealthy he becomes. However, the pedophile can be healthy and/or holy if he maintains and fosters chastity.

Pedophiles are persons like you and me. They are usually not incorrigible criminals, insane, or psychotic; they are likely to be concerned, normal, and productive citizens. We must treat pedophiles as brothers who are disordered sexually. Their problem does not come from willfulness; it is more akin to alcoholism. Those who are caught in the addiction of pedophilia ought to share their secret, heavy burden and seek help. The way to freedom includes being biologically sound, the limitation of contact with minors and increased involvement with peers, psychological insight, the learning of coping mechanisms, and a "let go and let God" attitude. These will give pedophiles the power to live chaste, healthy, and holy lives.

Epilogue

The recurrent theme of this book has been wholistic sexuality. Developing oneself wholistically involves seeing, thinking of, judging, feeling, appreciating, and enjoying sexuality from the lived integration of the physical, psychosocial, spiritual, and aesthetic dimensions of one's experience. The focus here has been practical: an integrative approach simply results in healthy and happy living. To settle for being less than whole can indeed evoke short-term gains, but at the price of long-term losses. Fragmented sexuality is commonly advocated and practiced today; it does not promote healthy virtues such as lasting dignity, integrity, serenity, and love.

Special emphasis has been placed on the spirituality of sexuality and on the sexuality of spirituality. To engage in sex without spirit is humanly understandable but not recommended—the consequences of spiritless sex are fragmentation, emptiness, and alienation. These are polar opposites of what healthy sexuality should produce. Spirituality without sexuality also brings negative consequences: despite the best of intentions, love, compassion, and counsel without embodiment are insipid, constricted, and distant. In either case, being less than whole wastes precious time and energy and fails to give us what we are searching for: the true growth of ourselves and others in freedom and serenity.

In short, we are both sexual and spiritual creatures; one without the other makes us less than God intends us to be. God calls us to use our minds and wills to maintain and nourish our sexual selves in congruence with authentic spiritual values. How we do this will be highly dependent on our vocational life-style—married, single, or vowed celibate—as well as individual and environmental factors. Whatever our situation, we are foolish to pursue less than wholistic sexual lives.

The saving grace in this adventure is that we are in it together. We are not isolated individuals alone in our efforts; rather, we are integral members of the same community of humankind. The more you and I grow in a healthy sexuality, the more we will positively impact and help each other.

It is eminently wise to acknowledge a Power that is greater than and yet intimately related to us—a God who will help us on the journey. To deny God, however we understand God, is to reject a Power that is the source of and means to healthy and holy sexual/spiritual living. To turn over our minds and wills to the care of God is a wise, practical decision. It will give us the vision and strength to become whole and holy mavericks who celebrate and live the unity of sex-and-spirit.

Terms Frequently Used

Aesthetic dimension. The dynamic unity of the physical, rational, and spiritual dimensions.

Affective sexuality. Feelings, moods, and emotions that lead to and/or involve intimacy.

Androgynous. Manifesting characteristics of both men and women.

Anima. An inner feminine part of the male personality.

Animus. An inner masculine part of the female personality.

Badness. Behavior that intends to violate love and/or community growth and welfare.

Bisexuality. Erotic desire for and/or genital gratification with both men and women.

Community. Being in union with; being an integral part of the same system: I-you-God are essentially interrelated.

Embodiment. Being incarnated; physical.

Femininity. The way a woman has learned to manifest herself and/or the cultural roles of being a woman.

Genital behavior. Actualizing one's genital desires with self or another.

Genitality. Genital feelings, thoughts, desires.

Genital sexuality. Behavior, thoughts, fantasies, desires, and feelings that activate the genital organs.

Gender. The condition of being primarily female or male.

Goodness. Behavior that is congruent with and fosters healthy love.

Healthy. Behavior that is congruent with and fosters wholistic growth.

Heterosexual. A person who finds himself or herself oriented towards erotic preference for the other sex.

Heterosexuality. Sexual relationship—primary, affective, or genital—between a man and a woman.

Homosexual. A person who finds himself or herself oriented toward erotic preference for the same sex.

Homosexuality. Behavior that leads to or involves genital gratification with the same sex; homogenitality.

Homosocial. Primary and/or affective sexual involvement with the same sex.

Integration. To make whole; to perceive and appreciate the unity of body, mind, and spirit.

Intimacy. Self-disclosure and sharing; personal and interpersonal closeness.

Love. To choose (rationally and/or transrationally) to foster the well-being of community.

Madness. Being closed to experiences that are significant to and necessary for wholistic/healthy growth.

Masculinity. The way a man has learned to manifest himself and/or the cultural roles of being a man.

Negative defense mechanisms. Processes by which we protect ourselves against unpleasant or anxious feelings that threaten to expose an unacceptable part of ourselves; e.g., repression, denial, rationalization, etc.

Nonhealthy. A lack of healthiness or wholeness.

Normality. Maintaining oneself and coping effectively with the everyday demands of reality.

Normal madness. Functioning within the confines of normal society without pathological symptoms, but still being closed to realities (e.g. spiritual ones) necessary for healthy living.

Pedophilia. A sexual disorder in which a minor is the love object.

Physical dimension. The structure and dynamics of a person's embodied-incarnated self. The pre-rational lived body.

Pornography. Anything, particularly mass media, whose primary purpose is to excite us genitally.

Primary sexuality. How men and women experience reality because of nature and nurture.

Psychosocial dimension. The structure and dynamics of functional ego activities that center around task-oriented behavior, coping, and cognitive processes; the rational self.

Sex. The inherited conditions that predispose and codetermine how we primarily as men and women relate to reality.

Sexuality. How we relate to objects, events, and persons by virtue of being primarily men or women; due to both nature and nurture.

Spiritual dimension. The structure and dynamics of experiences rooted in mystery, paradox, transcendence, and communal harmony; the transrational self.

Spirituality. The art of maintaining and promoting good and transrational experiences.

Wholistic. The ongoing integration of the physical, psychosocial, and spiritual dimensions of human experience.

Bibliography

Avvento, Genarro P. *Sexuality: A Christian View*. Mystic, CT: Twenty-Third Publications, 1982.

Beatty, Melody. *Co-dependent No More*. Center City, MN: Hazelden Publishing, 1987.

Bloom, Lynn A., Karen Coburn, and Joan Pearlway. *The New Assertive Woman*. New York: Dell Publishing Co., 1976.

Brecher, Edward M. *Love, Sex and Aging*. Boston: Little, Brown and Co., Inc., 1986.

Buber, Martin. *I and Thou*. New York: Charles Scribner's Sons, 1958.

Bullough, Vern and Bullough, Bonnie. *Sin, Sickness, and Sanity: A History of Sexual Attitudes*. New York: New American Library, 1977.

Buytendijk, Frederik J. *Woman: A Contemporary View*. Translated by Denis J. Burrett. New York: Newman Press, 1968.

Carrington, Patricia. *Freedom in Meditation*. New York: Pace Publications, 1977.

Clark, Keith. *Being Sexual ... And Celibate*. Notre Dame, IN: Ave Maria Press, 1986.

Cook, Mark and Howells, Kevin, eds. *Adult Sexual Interest in Children*. San Diego: Academic Press, Inc., 1981.

Doyle, James A. *Sex and Gender: The Human Experience*. Dubuque, IA: Wm. C. Brown Group, 1985.

Dubay, Thomas. "Celibacy as Fullness," *Review for Religious*, January 1975, 88-100.

Fasteau, Marc Feigen. *The Male Machine*. New York: Dell Publishing Co., 1976.

Fromm, Erich. *The Art of Loving*. New York: Harper and Row Publishers, Inc., 1974.

Gagnon, John H. and Smith, Barbara. *Human Sexualities*. Glenview, IL: Scott, Foresman and Co., 1977.

Goergen, Donald. *The Sexual Celibate*. New York: Harper and Row Publishers, Inc., 1975.

Greer, Germaine. *The Female Eunuch*. New York: Bantam Books, 1972.

Grisez, Germain and Shaw, Russell. *Beyond the New Morality*. Notre Dame, IN: University of Notre Dame Press, 1980.

Groeschel, Benedict. *The Courage to be Chaste*. Mahwah, NJ: The Paulist Press, 1985.

Hammarskjold, Dag. *Markings*. Translated by Leif Sjoberg and W.H. Auden. New York: Alfred A. Knopf, Inc., 1964.

Harding, M. Esther. *The Way of All Women*. New York: Harper and Row Publishers, Inc., 1975.

Heidegger, Martin. *Being and Time*. Translated by John Macquarrie and Edward Robinson. New York: Harper and Row Publishers, Inc., 1962.

Johnson, Robert A. *HE: Understanding Masculine Psychology*. New York: Harper and Row Publishers, Inc., 1986.

Johnson, Robert A. *SHE: Understanding Feminine Psychology*. New York: Harper and Row Publishers, Inc., 1986.

Johnston, William. *Silent Music: The Silence of Meditation*. New York: Harper and Row Publishers, 1979.

Jung, C.G. *Psyche and Symbol*. Translated by Gary Baynes and R.F.C. Hull. New York: Doubleday, 1958.

Keane, Philip S. *Sexual Morality: A Catholic Perspective*. Mahwah, NJ: Paulist Press, 1978.

Kraft, William F. *The Search for the Holy*. Philadelphia: Westminster Press, 1971.

Laing, R.D. *The Politics of Experience*. New York: Pantheon Books, Inc., 1957.

Lakoff, Robin. *Language and Woman's Place*. New York: Harper and Row Publishers, Inc., 1975.

Luijpen, William A. *Existential Phenomenology*. Pittsburgh: Duquesne University Press, 1969.

Maslow, Abraham H. *Toward a Psychology of Being*. Princeton, NJ: D. Van Nostrand Co., 1968.

Masters, William H. and Johnson, Virginia E. *The Pleasure Bond: A New Look at Sexuality and Commitment*. Boston: Little, Brown and Co., Inc., 1975.

May, Rollo. *Love and Will*. New York: W.W. Norton and Co., 1969.

McCary, Stephen P. and McCary, James L. *Human Sexuality*. Third Edition. Belmont, CA: Wadsworth Publishing Co., 1984.

McNamara, William. *Mystical Passion: Spirituality for a Bored Society*. Mahwah, NJ: Paulist Press, 1977.

Norwood, Robin. *Women Who Love Too Much*. New York: Jeremy P. Tarcher, Inc., 1985.

O'Brien, Shirley J. *Why They Did It: Stories of Eight Convicted Child Molesters*. Springfield, IL: Charles C. Thomas, 1986.

Olds, Linda E. *Fully Human*. Englewood Cliffs, NJ: Prentice-Hall, Inc., 1981.

Oraison, Marc. *The Human Mystery of Sexuality*. Kansas City, MO: Sheed and Ward, 1967.

Pable, Martin W. "Psychology and Asceticism of Celibacy," *Review for Religious*, March 1975, 266-276.

Sullivan, Harry Stack. *The Interpersonal Theory of Psychiatry*. New York: W.W. Norton and Co., Inc., 1968.

Tillich, Paul. *Love, Power, and Justice*. New York: Oxford University Press, Inc., 1954.

Van Breemen, Peter G. "Unmarriageable for God's Sake," *Review for Religious*, November 1975, 839-45.

Van Kaam, Adrian. "The Fantasy of Romantic Love," *Modern Myth and Popular Fancies*. Pittsburgh: Duquesne University Press, 1961.

Von Hildebrand, Dietrich. *Man and Woman*. Ann Arbor, MI: UMI Research, 1966.

Weideger, Paula. *Menstruation and Menopause*. New York: Dell Publishing Co., 1977.

Weinberg, George. *Society and the Healthy Homosexual*. New York: Doubleday, 1973.

Williams, Juanita H. *Psychology of Women: Behavior in a Biosocial Context*. New York: W.W. Norton and Co., Inc., 1987.